Part One

786.92 BAK

The Complete Keyboard Player

LESSONS

by **Kenneth Baker**

SONGS

Part Two

Part Three

YOUR KEYBOARD

Although the actual layout of modern keyboards varies from model to model, the following features are standard:-

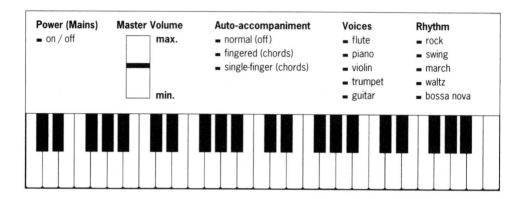

POWER (MAINS)

Turns the keyboard on or off. Most keyboards can run on batteries or from the mains, using a suitable transformer (see your owner's manual).

MASTER VOLUME

Controls the overall "loudness" of the instrument.
Usually in the form of a "slider", which can be set anywhere from "minimum" to "maximum".

AUTO-ACCOMPANIMENT

Adds an accompaniment to your melody – AUTOMATICALLY.

VOICES (INSTRUMENTS, ORCHESTRA, SOLO)

A selection of sounds and effects to add colour to your melody.

RHYTHM

Adds drums to your performance.

SITTING AT YOUR KEYBOARD

Set up your keyboard on its own stand or on a table of medium height. Sit facing the centre of the instrument and adjust your seat so that your arms are level with the keyboard, or sloping down slightly towards it:-

Support your hands from the wrists. Imagine that you are holding a rather fragile ball, and curve your fingers lightly around it:-

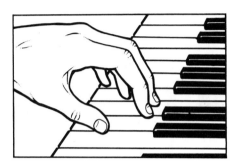

With the tips of your fingers cover any five adjacent white notes in each hand:-

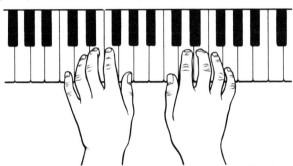

This is your normal, most relaxed playing position. After all fingering and hand changes during a piece, you should return to this position.

FINGER NUMBERS

Your fingers are numbered OUTWARDS from the thumbs, like this:-

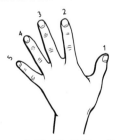

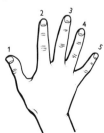

L.H. (Left Hand)   R.H. (Right Hand)

2 WARM UP

Switch on your keyboard now and turn up the Master Volume control to about halfway. Locate your AUTO section (could be called "Auto Bass Chord", or "Auto-accompaniment") and switch it to NORMAL or OFF:-

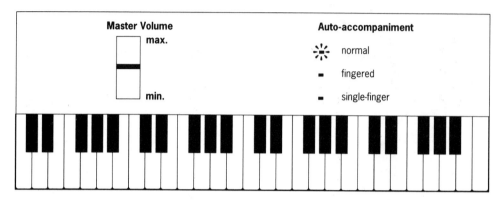

Check that you have a sound on your keyboard (any sound will do). If there is no sound, check that all subsidiary volume controls are up. Run the back of your right hand along the keys from left to right, and note the sounds progressing from LOW to HIGH. Now run your right hand thumb nail along the keys in the opposite direction (from right to left), and note the sounds progressing from HIGH to LOW. Locate your VOICES (INSTRUMENTS) section, and select "piano":-

Play a few notes at random and listen to the sound of the piano. Try adding any special "effects" you might have, such as:-

VIBRATO

An oscillation, or "wobble" of the note(s).

SUSTAIN

Causes the note(s) to ring on.

REVERBERATION (REVERB)

Adds "echo".

STEREO (or STEREO CHORUS)

Transfers the sound rapidly from speaker to speaker.

Experiment with other voices in the same way.

Note that the "violin" sounds best in the upper part of the keyboard, because this is where a real violin would play, whilst the "trombone" – to be realistic – needs to be played in the low to middle register.

NOW LET'S PLAY RHYTHM

Your keyboard has a built in drummer, and he's raring to go! There are various rhythms available to you, such as ROCK, SWING, BOSSA NOVA, MARCH, POP, WALTZ, etc. These rhythms can run at virtually any speed (tempo), all controlled by you. In your RHYTHM or STYLE section now, select ROCK, and press the start button:-

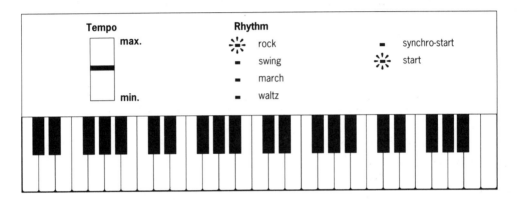

Listen to this Rock rhythm for a while, then try speeding it up and slowing it down, using your TEMPO control (sometimes marked simply: $+$ and $-$).

Press another rhythm button now, say SWING, and hear the rhythm pattern change. Speed up and slow down this Swing rhythm ad lib., then stop it, by pressing the START button again.

SYNCHRO-START*

This is another, very useful method of starting the drums. Locate and press your SYNCHRO-START button now. Nothing will happen at first (though you may see a flashing light, indicating the speed of the rhythm that is to come).

Play any note in the bottom left hand section of your keyboard, and your drummer will start to play. Stop the rhythm by pressing the START button again.

* Not all keyboards have "synchro-start".

3 BLACK AND WHITE NOTES

Your keyboard has a number of black and white keys*. The black keys are divided into groups of twos and threes, and these same groups repeat all along the keyboard:-

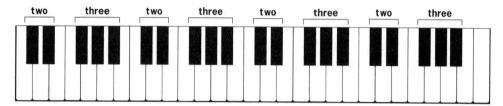

You need these black key groups to locate the white notes.

YOUR FIRST WHITE NOTE: C

C is a very commonly used white note. The C's lie directly to the left of each of the "two blacks":-

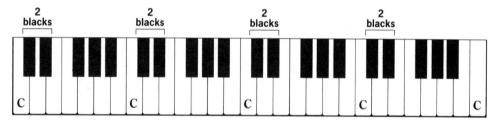

Punch out your C "stickers" now (included with this book), and place one, without sticking it, on each of your C notes.

Check the position of these C's in relation to the groups of two black notes, then remove the stickers and see if you can locate the C's without them.

THE OTHER WHITE NOTES

The musical alphabet runs from A to G, and then repeats itself over and over again. So there are **ONLY SEVEN WHITE NOTES TO LEARN**:-

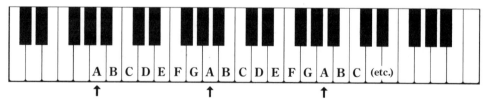

*The exact number of keys varies from model to model.

YOUR SECOND WHITE NOTE: G

The G notes lie here, within the "three" black note groups:-

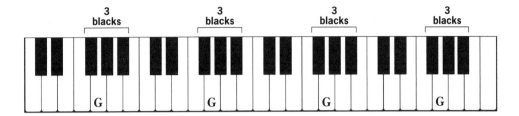

Punch out your G stickers now, and place them (without sticking) on all the G notes.
Check out their position, then remove the stickers and locate all the G's without them.

SPLITTING THE KEYBOARD

Return to your AUTO section again, and switch on "single-finger chords".

Your keyboard is now divided into two distinct sections:-

A **MELODY** section

An **ACCOMPANIMENT** section

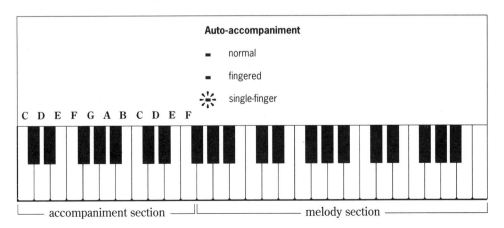

ACCOMPANIMENT SECTION

The Accompaniment Section of your keyboard is situated at the bottom end (left hand side) of your keyboard. It has note names (letters) printed above it, with an arrow, or bracket, to show where the section ends*. Check to see that you have "single-finger chords" selected, then play any note in your accompaniment section, using your left hand (finger 2, say). You are now hearing a CHORD (three notes playing together), plus (probably), a single bass note.

Play a few more single notes at random in your accompaniment section and listen to the sounds of the chords which your keyboard is producing automatically.

(NOTE: You may have to activate your Rhythm Section to make these single-finger chords work. If so, select any rhythm, say "rock", and press START.)

[C] AND [G] CHORDS

Now, in your accompaniment section, let's learn two specific chords. Do you remember how the note "C" looks, in relation to its two adjacent black keys?

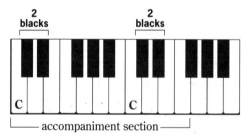

Check that you still have "single-finger chords" set on your keyboard, then play the UPPER C, shown above, with your left hand 2nd finger:-

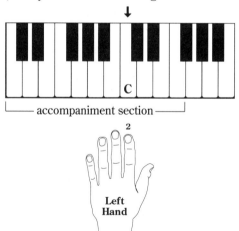

* The extent of the accompaniment section can vary from model to model.

You can check your C with the letters printed on the fascia of the keyboard.

You are now playing a chord of C, which is written in a box, like this:- C

Do you remember how "G" looks, in relation to its three neighbouring black keys?

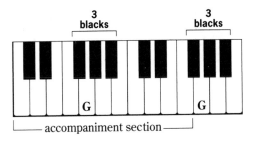

Play the LOWER G (shown above) with your left hand 5th finger:-

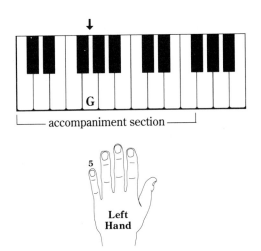

Check your G against the letters on the fascia.

You are now playing a chord of G, written like this:- G

5 ADDING RHYTHM TO YOUR CHORDS

In the RHYTHM section of your keyboard, set "Rock" and "Synchro-start".
(Leave single-finger chords set in the AUTO section.) In the Accompaniment Section
of your keyboard, play C with your left hand 2nd finger:-

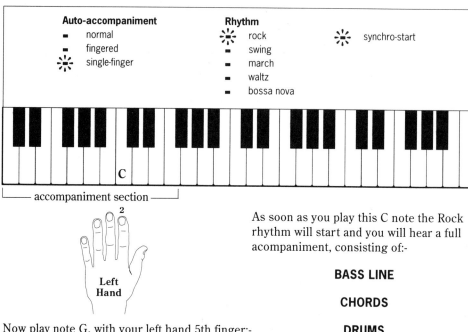

As soon as you play this C note the Rock
rhythm will start and you will hear a full
acompaniment, consisting of:-

BASS LINE

CHORDS

Now play note G, with your left hand 5th finger:-

DRUMS

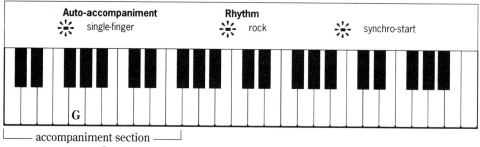

The accompaniment pattern will now change to a chord of G . Listen to this new chord
for a while, then change back to C . Feel free to lift your finger once you have played
each chord note. The rhythm will continue indefinitely while you get ready for the next
chord note. Try a new rhythm pattern now, say "Bossa Nova", and alternate between the
two chords, C and G at your leisure.

6 BEATS AND BARS

When you were playing there did you feel the natural pulse of the music? Underlying most popular music there are pulses, or "beats", which have a regularly recurring accent:-

beats:– 1 2 3 4 1 2 3 4 1 2 3 4 (etc.)
       >   >   >

When writing this down, vertical lines, called "bar lines", are placed in front of each accented beat:-

beats:– |1 2 3 4 |1 2 3 4 |1 2 3 4 | (etc.)
      >   >   >
   ↑   ↑   ↑   ↑
bar lines

As well as denoting the natural accents of the piece, these bar lines divide the music up into "bars", or "measures":-

    bar (measure) 1   bar 2   bar 3

beats:– |1 2 3 4 |1 2 3 4 |1 2 3 4 | (etc.)
     >   >   >

SPACEMAN – ACCOMPANIMENT

Here is your first piece:-

SPACEMAN

Single-finger chords: on
Rhythm: rock
Tempo: medium

     C finger 2   G finger 5   C   G

beats: ‖: 1 2 3 4 |1 2 3 4 |1 2 3 4 |1 2 3 4 :‖
                                        ↑

                        REPEAT SIGN
                 (go back to the opposite
                 facing sign, and repeat)

For the accompaniment to this piece you need two chords: C and G . They are to be played in the ACCOMPANIMENT SECTION of your keyboard, with your left hand, finger 2 on C , finger 5 on G . You hold the C chord for one bar (4 beats), then change to a G chord for one bar, then go back to a C chord for one bar, and so on. If you have the audio which accompanies this book, listen to "*SPACEMAN – ACCOMPANIMENT*" now.

7 SPLITTING THE KEYBOARD 2 – THE MELODY SECTION

As you learnt earlier, when you select "single-finger chords" in your AUTO section, you split your keyboard into two sections:-

single-finger chords: on

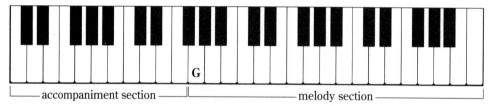

└── accompaniment section ──┘└────── melody section ──────┘

In the MELODY SECTION (which usually begins at G, but can vary from model to model – see your Owner's Manual), you play the MELODY, or TUNE of the piece, with your right hand. The Voices, or Instruments (flute, piano, violin, etc.), apply only to the MELODY SECTION, since, when the keyboard is split, the Accompaniment Section has a fixed sound.

SPACEMAN – MELODY

This first simple melody consists of only two notes: C and G. In your "voices" section select some kind of "spacey" sound, such as COSMIC, or SYNTH.

SPACEMAN

```
                                              G  G  G  G
                           C  C  C  C
            G  G  G  G                         (etc., up and down)
         |C  C  C  C  |G  G  G  G  |C  C  C  C  |G  G  G  G  |
beats:-  |1  2  3  4  |1  2  3  4  |1  2  3  4  |1  2  3  4  |
```

As you see, the C note is played four times, then the G note is played four times. This is then repeated on the various higher C's and G's, right to the top of the keyboard, then down again. To save complications, use your right hand finger 2 throughout.
Start on your most central C (MIDDLE C), and finish on the G immediately to its right:-

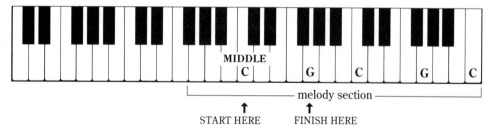

└────────── melody section ──────────┘
        ↑   ↑
   START HERE   FINISH HERE

Don't forget, you will be adding an accompaniment later, so *PLAY RHYTHMICALLY*.

If you have the audio which accompanies this book, listen to "*SPACEMAN –MELODY*" now.

SPACEMAN – BOTH HANDS

Now that you can play both the accompaniment and melody of *Spaceman*, try the piece with both hands together.

Here it is written out in simple form:-

SPACEMAN Kenneth Baker

Suggested registration (sound setting): cosmic or synth
Rhythm: rock
Tempo: medium
Single-finger chords: on

C	G	C	G

(play ascending and descending)

beats: ‖: C C C C | G G G G | C C C C | G G G G :‖
         1 2 3 4   1 2 3 4   1 2 3 4   1 2 3 4

If you have the audio which accompanies this book, listen to *"SPACEMAN – BOTH HANDS"* now.

SPACEMAN – VARIATION

This time, in the melody of *Spaceman*, instead of "jumping" from C to G, then G to C, and so on, you are going to SLIDE:-

SPACEMAN Kenneth Baker

beats: ‖: C C C C | G G G G | C C C C | G G G G :‖
         1 2 3 4   1 2 3 4   1 2 3 4   1 2 3 4

Play your four C's as before, then turn your right hand 2nd finger over, and slide rapidly up the intervening white notes until you reach G. Play the four G's as written, then slide up again to the next C, and so on. This sliding technique is called a GLISSANDO (Gliss. for short). On the way down the keyboard you will probably have to change your finger angle to do the glissandi, or, if you wish, you can use your right thumb nail instead.

If you have the audio which accompanies this book, listen to *"SPACEMAN – VARIATION"* now.

15

WHITE ROSE OF ATHENS – ACCOMPANIMENT

The accompaniment to this song uses the same two chords as *Spaceman*: C and G, but each chord lasts longer:-

WHITE ROSE OF ATHENS

Words by Norman Newell. Music by Manos Hadjidakis. Additional words by Archie Bleyer

Single-finger chords: on
Rhythm: 8 beat
Tempo: fairly fast
Synchro-start: on

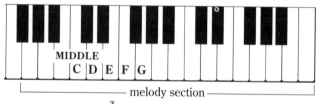

	C finger 2								G finger 5							
beats:	1	2	3	4	1	2	3	4	1	2	3	4	1	2	3	4

Set up your keyboard as shown above (single-finger chords: on, etc.). Play the first chord C in your Accompaniment Section. The rhythm will start automatically, due to the "synchro-start". Count the beats, following the natural pulse of the music. After two bars (8 beats in all), change to a chord of G and allow this chord to continue for a further FOUR bars (16 beats in all). After that change back to C for a further four bars, and so on, to the end of the song.

If you have the audio which accompanies this book, listen to "*WHITE ROSE OF ATHENS – ACCOMPANIMENT*" now.

WHITE ROSE OF ATHENS – MELODY

To play the melody of *White Rose Of Athens* you need the following five notes:-

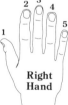

You may place stickers on these five notes if you wish.

Here are those notes written:-

TREBLE CLEF
(used for right hand notes)

STAVE
(5 horizontal
lines)

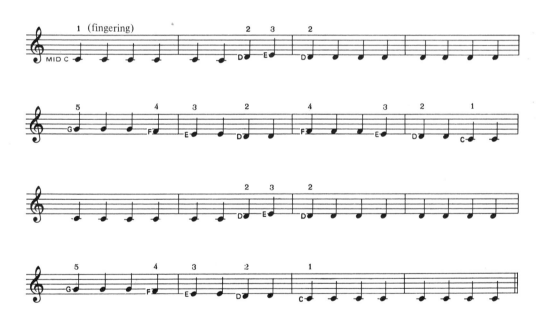

MIDDLE C   D   E   F   G

As you see, the five notes, which are next door on the keyboard, climb up a sort of musical ladder, using various rungs and the spaces in between them. MIDDLE C is a rather low note, and since there are only five rungs available on the stave, MIDDLE C has to stand below the stave on a little rung of its own. These little rungs (drawn above or below the stave as necessary) are called "Ledger Lines".

Here now is a simplified version of *White Rose Of Athens,* written down in musical notation:

WHITE ROSE OF ATHENS

Words by Norman Newell. Music by Manos Hadjidakis. Additional words by Archie Bleyer

Suggested registration: bouzouki (or guitar)

This song starts on MIDDLE C, played with your right thumb (finger 1). The Middle C note plays six times in all, then the melody moves up by step (i.e. line, to space, to line) through "D" and "E", returning then to the D note, which plays eight times. The second half of the song is similar to the first.

Work through the above version of *White Rose Of Athens* in your own time, noticing all the repeated notes, and the various movements up or down "by step", then listen to this song on your audio (if you have one) to compare results.

LONG AND SHORT NOTES

In *Spaceman*, and the previous "simplified" version of *White Rose Of Athens*, all the melody notes were the same length, and followed the beat exactly. These "beat" notes, called "quarter notes" or "crotchets", are written like this:-

WHITE ROSE OF ATHENS

However, tunes do not slavishly follow the beat like this as a rule: to make things more interesting they employ a mixture of LONG and SHORT notes:-

TIME NOTE CHART

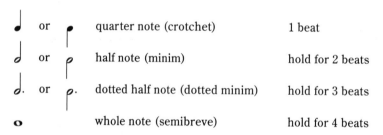

In the final, correct version of *White Rose Of Athens* (page 19), some of the melody notes must be held down LONGER:–

WHITE ROSE OF ATHENS

In BAR 1, above, the "C" note is played on beat 1, then held down for a further two beats (beats 2 and 3), while in BAR 3, above, the "D" note is played on beat 1, then held down for a further SEVEN beats, making 8 beats in all. This extension of the "D" note is made possible by the use of a "tie" – a curved line joining two (or more) notes of the same pitch (two "D's", two "E's", etc.).

Work through the whole of *White Rose Of Athens*, (on page 19) now, right hand only, counting your beats and striking or holding down your notes as indicated by the music. When you have mastered the right hand, add the left hand chords and listen to your audio (if you have one) to check your results.

WHITE ROSE OF ATHENS

Words by Norman Newell. Music by Manos Hadjidakis.
Additional words by Archie Bleyer.

Suggested registration: bouzouki (or guitar)

Rhythm: 8 beat
Tempo: fairly fast (♩ = 116)*
Synchro-start: on

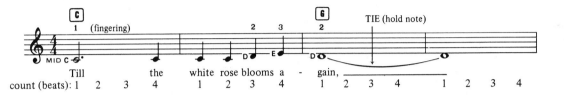

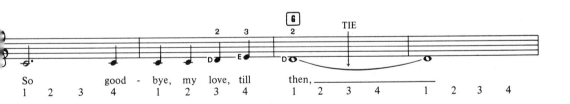

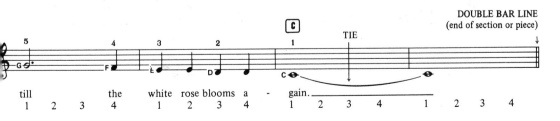

*__METRONOME MARKING.__ A metronome is an instrument which indicates the speed (tempo) of a piece of music. Some modern keyboards have a metronome built in. If yours doesn't, you can buy a metronome, if you wish, from your local music dealer.

12 FINGERED CHORDS

Although it is entirely up to you, it would probably be better in the long run to learn to form real chords in your left hand. To do this switch on FINGERED (CHORDS) in your Auto Accompaniment section, and play as follows:-

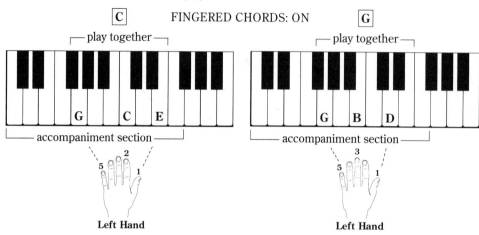

Practise moving from C to G and back, using the correct fingers, as shown. Since the bottom note, G, is common to both chords, it is good practice to hold it down during the changes.

With Rock rhythm selected, press rhythm START and change your chord on each beat 1, like this:-

Rhythm: rock
Tempo: medium
($\downarrow$ = 112)

count: ‖: 4/4   1   2   3   4 │1   2   3   4 │1   2   3   4 │1   2   3   4 :‖

C   G   C   G

NEW CHORD: F

single-finger method
SINGLE-FINGER CHORDS: ON
F

fingered chord method
FINGERED CHORDS: ON
F

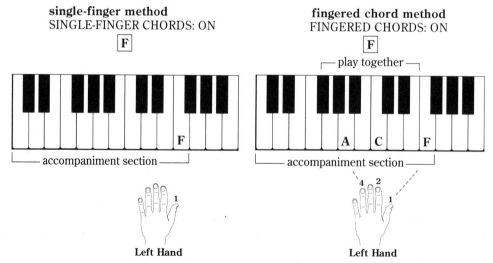

Practise moving from F to C and back, first without rhythm, then with rhythm:-

Rhythm: rock
Tempo: medium
($\downarrow$ = 112)

count:|: $\frac{4}{4}$ F   1   2   3   4 | C   1   2   3   4 | F   1   2   3   4 | C   1   2   3   4 :|

When playing as "fingered" chords, hold down the middle note, C, throughout.

Now practise moving through F , C , and G , like this:-

Rhythm: rock
Tempo: medium
($\downarrow$ = 112)

count:|: $\frac{4}{4}$ F   1   2   3   4 | C   1   2   3   4 | G   1   2   3   4 | C   1   2   3   4 :|

The next two songs: *Bye Bye Love*, and *World*, were big hits for the Everly Brothers, and the Bee Gees respectively. Both songs feature the new chord, F . Practise left and right hands separately, first without rhythm, then with rhythm. When you are totally proficient, put both hands together.

MUSICAL TIES

As we saw in *White Rose Of Athens*, page 18 ff., any note(s) in music may be made to last longer by the use of a TIE. You meet ties next in *World*:-

WORLD (page 23)

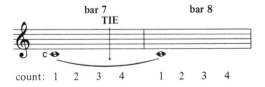

bar 7   bar 8
TIE

count: 1   2   3   4   1   2   3   4

Play the C note on beat 1, then hold it down for two whole bars (eight beats in all).

PLAYING *LEGATO*

LEGATO is an Italian word, meaning "smooth", "joined up". As you play through the melodies of the next two songs, walk very precisely from finger to finger, releasing the old finger EXACTLY as the new finger goes down. There should be no breaks in sound between the notes, nor ugly overlaps either. This joined-up style of playing is called LEGATO. You always play legato, unless the music is marked otherwise.

BYE BYE LOVE

Words & Music by Felice and Boudleaux Bryant

Suggested registration: clarinet

Rhythm: swing
Tempo: medium (♩ = 132)
Synchro-start: on

WORLD

Words & Music by Barry Gibb, Robin Gibb and Maurice Gibb

Suggested registration: horn

Rhythm: rock
Tempo: medium (♩ = 112)
Synchro-start: on

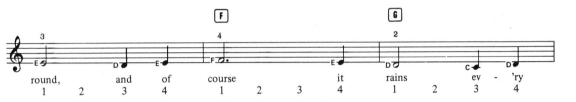

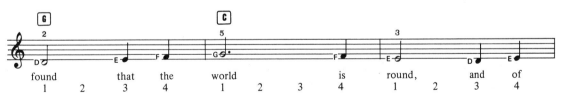

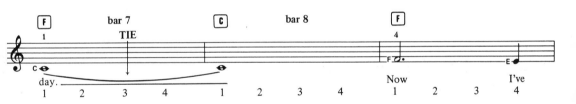

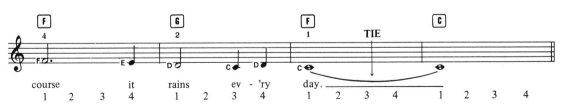

13 PICK-UP NOTES

Songs do not always begin on beat 1. In your next song, *One More Night*, by Phil Collins, the melody actually begins on beat 2:-

ONE MORE NIGHT (page 25)

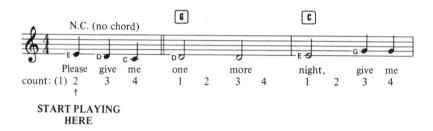

The three preliminary notes at the beginning of *One More Night* are called PICK-UP NOTES. Beats missing from the pick-up bar appear (usually) in the last bar of the song:-

ONE MORE NIGHT (end)

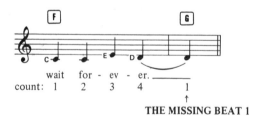

This means that you can go around the song again if you wish, keeping the beats intact.

NOTE: It is usual to play "no chord" (written N.C.) during pick-up notes.

ONE MORE NIGHT

Words & Music by Phil Collins

Suggested registration: guitar

Rhythm: rock
Tempo: quite slow (♩ = 92)
Synchro-start: on

14 THREE NEW NOTES: A, B, C, FOR RIGHT HAND

FINGERING THE NEW NOTES

Now that you are moving beyond the original playing range of your five fingers, new fingering techniques will have to be adopted if the music is to remain LEGATO.

BLOWIN' IN THE WIND (page 29, last two bars)

Don't jump here; STRETCH OUT for the high C.

OH, LONESOME ME (page 30, bars 9, 10 and 11)

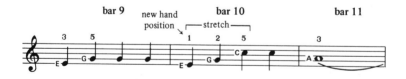

After playing the last "G" in bar 9, squeeze your hand together in order to get your thumb onto the next note, E. Now STRETCH OUT to encompass the next two notes (G and C).

As soon as you have completed any stretching movements in a song, let your hand return to its normal, relaxed five finger playing position (see picture on page 5).

RESTS

Silences are often called for in music. In order to indicate these, symbols called "rests" are used. Each of the Time Notes has its own rest:-

TIME NOTE		REST (SILENCE)	LASTING
♩	quarter note (crotchet)	𝄽	1 beat
♩	half note (minim)	▬	2 beats
♩.	dotted half note (dotted minim)	▬.	3 beats
𝅝	whole note (semibreve)	▬	4 beats, or one whole bar, regardless of time signature.

Rests are used mainly for musical or dramatic reasons. However, they are also useful for moving your hand from one part of the keyboard to another:-

OH, LONESOME ME (page 30, bars 12 and 13)

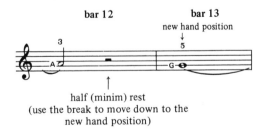

bar 12   bar 13
new hand position

half (minim) rest
(use the break to move down to the
new hand position)

WALTZ TIME

So far all our songs have been in four-time ($\frac{4}{4}$). However, many popular songs have THREE beats to the bar, rather than four. Songs in $\frac{3}{4}$ time (3 "quarter notes" per bar), are called "Waltzes". *Tales Of The Unexpected*, on page 32, is a waltz.

BLOWIN' IN THE WIND

Words & Music by Bob Dylan

Suggested registration: oboe

Rhythm: 8 beat
Tempo: medium ($\quad$ = 104)
Synchro-start: on

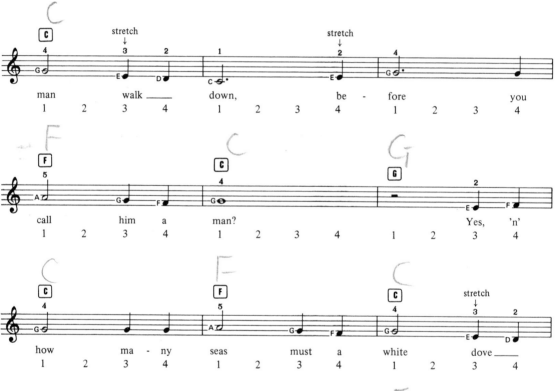

*The **VERSE** is that part of the song which contains the bulk of the narrative. It is usually sung by a solo singer.

** **CHORUS:** That part of the song where everybody joins in.

OH, LONESOME ME

Words & Music by Don Gibson

Suggested registration: violin

Rhythm: swing
Tempo: fast (♩ = 176)
Synchro-start: on

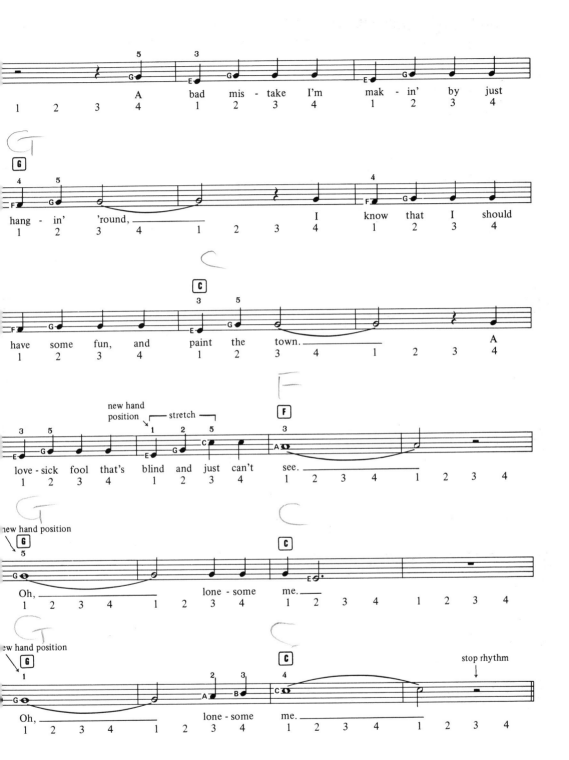

15 NEW RIGHT HAND NOTE: D

NEW NOTE

TALES OF THE UNEXPECTED
(Theme from)

By Ron Grainer

Suggested registration: marimba (or harpsichord)

Rhythm: waltz
Tempo: fast (♩ = 192)
Synchro-start: on

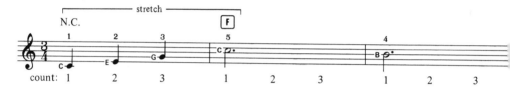

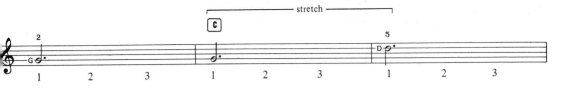

stretch

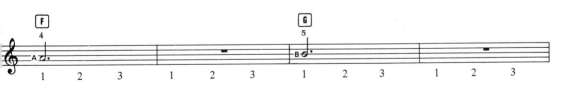

new hand position

stop rhythm

16 EIGHTH NOTES (QUAVERS)

The eighth note, or quaver, is another sort of time note:-

eighth notes (quavers)

Eighth notes move twice as fast as your basic quarter note (crotchet) beat:-

In other words, each eighth note is worth HALF A BEAT. If you say the word "and" in between your beat numbers you will get the feel of the eighth note:-

example:-

count: 1   2   3   4   1   and   2   and   3   and   4   and

Keep your basic beats very regular here, then fit the quaver notes *exactly* in between them.

Like all the other time notes, the eighth note has its own rest:-

eighth (quaver) rest	equivalent to	lasting
		1/2 beat

Count eighth "rests" in exactly the same way that you would count eighth notes:-

SUPER TROUPER (page 35)

bar 7

bar 8
eighth rest
↓

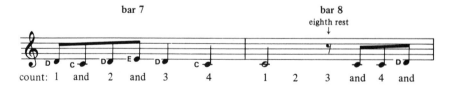

count: 1   and   2   and   3   4   1   2   3   and   4   and

34

SUPER TROUPER

Words & Music by Benny Andersson and Bjorn Ulvaeus

Suggested registration: trumpet

Rhythm: rock
Tempo: medium (♩ = 104)
Synchro-start: on

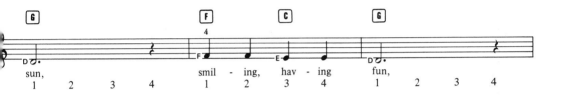

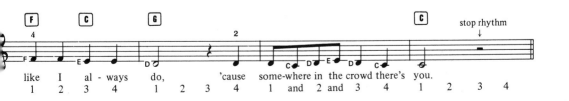

ANNIE'S SONG

Words & Music by John Denver

Suggested registration: flute

Rhythm: waltz
Tempo: medium (♩ = 120)
Synchro-start: on

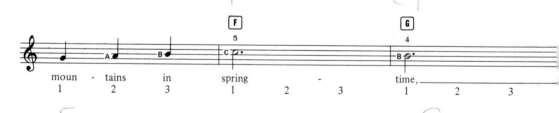

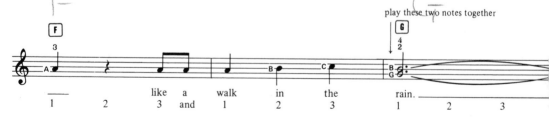

17 LEGATO AND STACCATO

As you know, LEGATO means "joined up", or "connected". When you play legato, you move smoothly from finger to finger, leaving no gaps between notes.

Notes which are to be played legato are indicated on the music by a curved line, called a "slur", or "phrase mark":-

BIRDIE SONG / BIRDIE DANCE (page 39)

SLUR
(play legato)

When there are no slurs, or other markings to the contrary, play LEGATO.

STACCATO means "cut short". It is the opposite of "legato". Release the note as soon as you have played it, using a "pecking" movement of the hand. Notes which are to be played staccato are indicated on the music by dots above, or below the note(s):-

BIRDIE SONG / BIRDIE DANCE (page 39)

STACCATO DOTS
(cut the notes short)

BIRDIE SONG / BIRDIE DANCE

Words & Music by Werner Thomas and Terry Rendall

Suggested registration: banjo

Rhythm: cha-cha (or rock)
Tempo: medium (♩ = 120)
Synchro-start: on

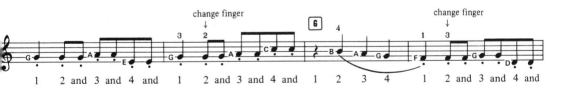

NEW RIGHT HAND NOTES: E, F, G

LA BAMBA

Adapted and arranged by Ritchie Valens

Suggested registration: flute

Rhythm: latin (or samba)
Tempo: fairly fast (♩ = 132)
Synchro-start: on

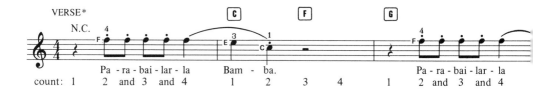

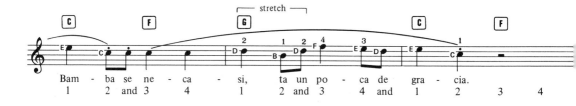

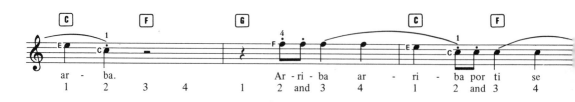

* The **VERSE** is that part of the song which contains the bulk of the narrative. It is usually sung by a solo singer.

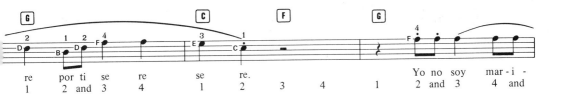

re por ti se re se re.
1 2 and 3 4 1 2 3 4 1

Yo no soy mar - i -
2 and 3 4 and

ne - ro.
1 2 3 4 1

Yo no soy mar - i - ne - ro, soy cap - i -
2 and 3 4 and 1 2 and 3 4

squeeze together — stretch — change finger flute to brass ensemble

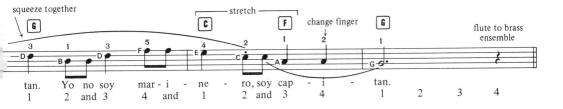

tan. Yo no soy mar - i - ne - ro, soy cap - i - tan.
1 2 and 3 4 and 1 2 and 3 4 1 2 3 4

CHORUS**
stretch stretch

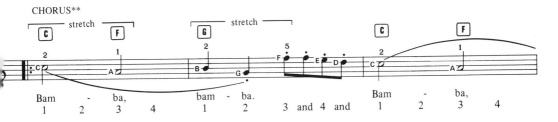

Bam - ba, bam - ba. Bam - ba,
1 2 3 4 1 2 3 and 4 and 1 2 3 4

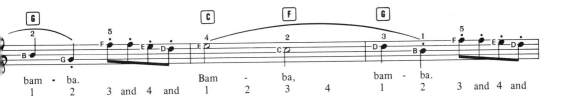

bam - ba. Bam - ba, bam - ba.
1 2 3 and 4 and 1 2 3 4 1 2 3 and 4 and

(If no foot volume pedal available, finish here)

Repeat and Fade

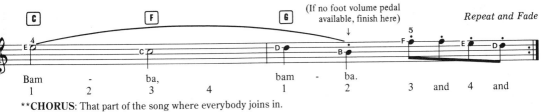

Bam - ba, bam - ba.
1 2 3 4 1 2 3 and 4 and

**CHORUS: That part of the song where everybody joins in.

SEVENTH CHORDS

The three chords you have played so far: ⬚C⬚ , ⬚G⬚ , and ⬚F⬚ , are all "major" chords. SEVENTH chords are variations of major chords. When using the "single-finger" chord method, there are various ways of forming "sevenths". Your Owner's Manual will tell you exactly how to form 7ths on your particular instrument, but the first two diagrams below show two possibilities:-

CHORD OF ⬚G⬚ 7

Using single-finger chord method – SINGLE-FINGER CHORDS: ON

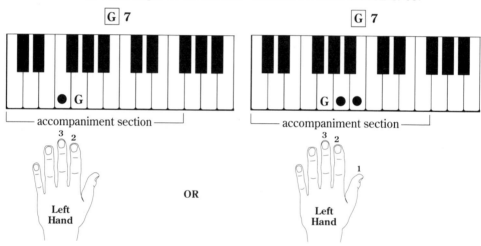

OR

Play G, together with any white note to its LEFT.

Play G, together with any two notes to its RIGHT.

Using fingered chord method:- FINGERED CHORDS: ON

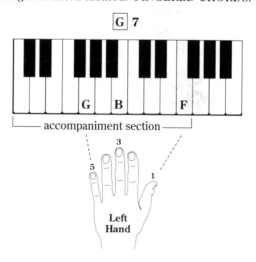

CHORD OF D 7

Using single-finger chord method – SINGLE-FINGER CHORDS: ON

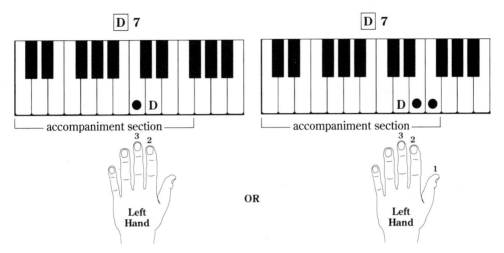

Play D, together with any white note to its LEFT.

OR

Play D, together with any two notes to its RIGHT.

Using fingered chord method – FINGERED CHORDS: ON

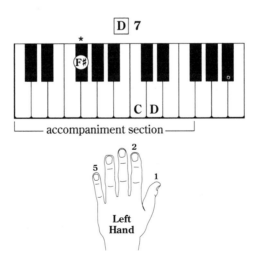

* Sharps and flats will be explained in Part Two. For now simply play the black note indicated.

SOMETIMES WHEN WE TOUCH

Words & Music by Dan Hill and Barry Mann

Suggested registration: oboe

Rhythm: 8 beat
Tempo: fairly slow (♩ = 92)
Synchro-start: on

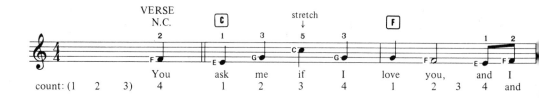

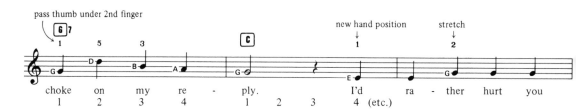

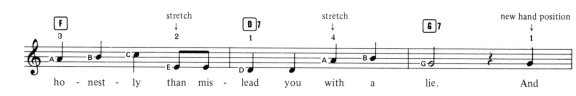

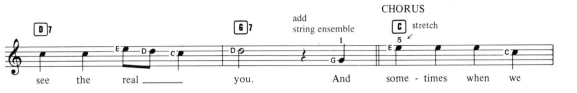

see the real _____ you.   And   some - times   when   we

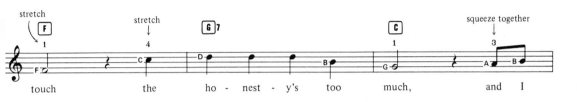

touch   the   ho - nest - y's   too   much,   and   I

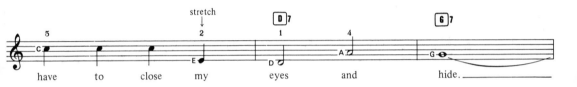

have   to   close   my   eyes   and   hide. _____

_____   I   wan - na   hold   you   till   I   die,   till   we

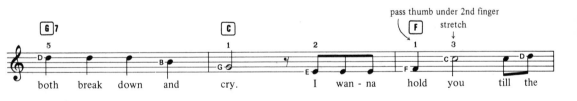

both   break   down   and   cry.   I   wan - na   hold   you   till   the

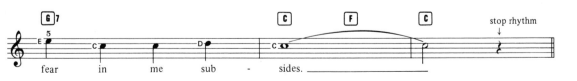

fear   in   me   sub - sides. _____

DAL SEGNO AL FINE (D.S. al Fine)

DAL SEGNO means "repeat from the sign":- 𝄋

FINE is the end of the piece.

DAL SEGNO AL FINE (D.S. al Fine) means go back to the sign: 𝄋 and play through the same music as before until you reach the word "Fine". This is where the piece ends.

I'D LIKE TO TEACH THE WORLD TO SING

Words & Music by Roger Cook, Roger Greenaway, Billy Backer and Billy Davis

Suggested registration: vibraphone

Rhythm: swing
Tempo: medium (♩ = 120)
Synchro-start: on

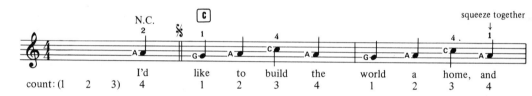

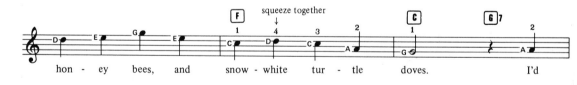

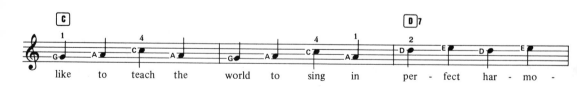

ny,   I'd like to hold   it   in   my arms, and

keep it com - pa - ny. That's the song   I   hear,
1   2 and 3   4   1   2   3   4

(stop rhythm last time)

let the world sing to - day. ___ 2   3   4   1   2   3   4   (etc.)
1   2 and 3   4 and 1   A

song of peace that ech - oes on, and nev - er goes a -

way.   Put your hand   in   my hand,

let's be - gin to - day.   Put your hand in

my hand,   help me find the way.   I'd

20 CONGRATULATIONS

Congratulations on completing Part One of 'The Complete Keyboard Player'.

In Part Two you will:-

- learn about sharps and flats

- increase the range of your melody playing

- learn new left hand chords, including "minor" chords

- experiment with new sounds and rhythms.

Till then your last piece in this book is:-

LET IT BE

Words & Music by John Lennon and Paul McCartney

Suggested registration: piano

Rhythm: rock
Tempo: slow (♩ = 66)
Synchro-start: on

The Complete Keyboard Player

by **Kenneth Baker**

In Part Two of The Complete Keyboard Player you take a giant step forward in reading musical notation.

Side by side with the single-finger chords, you continue your study of 'fingered' chords, by far the most rewarding aspect of left hand accompaniment playing.

As the book progresses you play more and more fill-ins, double notes, and chords with your right hand, which helps give you that 'professional' sound.

Although Part Two (like Part One) is designed basically as a 'teach yourself' method, teachers everywhere will find it ideal for training tomorrow's electronic keyboard players.

The optional matching CD or cassette, on which you can hear the author playing all the songs from the book, will help you to learn even faster!

SHARPS, FLATS, AND NATURALS

This sign is a sharp: ♯

When you see a sharp written alongside a note, play the nearest available key (black or white) to the RIGHT of that note:-

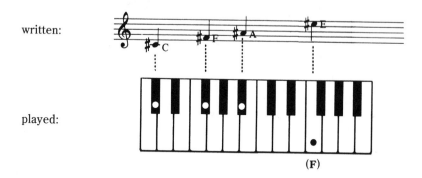

Note: E sharp is simply an alternative way of writing "F".

This sign is a flat: ♭

When you see a flat written alongside a note, play the nearest available key (black or white) to the LEFT of that note:-

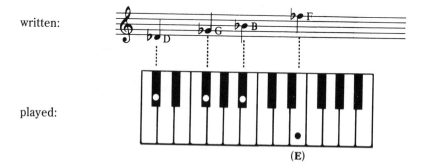

Note: F flat is simply an alternative way of writing "E".

When a sharp or flat is written it continues as a sharp or flat right through the bar:-

At the next bar, however, everything returns to normal:-

Apart from at the new bar, a sharp or flat may be cancelled any time by a sign called a "natural", ♮ :-

Look out for sharps, flats, and naturals in the pieces which follow.

GET BACK

Words & Music by John Lennon & Paul McCartney

Suggested registration: electric guitar

Rhythm: jazz organ
Tempo: medium (♩ = 120)
Synchro-start: on

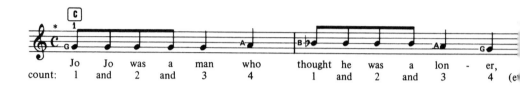

Jo   Jo   was   a   man   who   thought   he   was   a   lon - er,

count: 1   and   2   and   3   4   1   and   2   and   3   4   (e

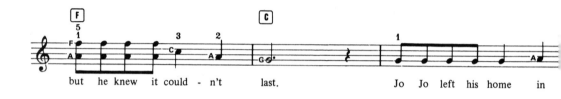

but   he   knew   it   could - n't   last.   Jo   Jo   left   his   home   in

Tuc - son,   Ar - i - zo - na,   for   some   Cal - i - for - nia   grass.   Get   ba

change finger on G

Get   back!   Get   back   to   where   you   once   be

longed. ___   Get   back!   Get   back!   Get

*COMMON TIME. An alternative way of writing 4/4.

back to where you once be - longed___ Sweet Lo - ret - ta Mod - ern

thought she was a wo - man, but she was an - oth - er man.

All the girls a - round her say she's got it com - ing, but she gets it while she

can. Get back! Get back! Get

back to where you once be - longed___ Get back! Get back!

Get back to where you once be - longed. ___

*Pause (Fermata). Hold the note(s) longer than written (at the discretion of the performer).

FOR ONCE IN MY LIFE

Words by Ronald Miller
Music by Orlando Murden

Suggested registration: piano + string ensemble
Arpeggio optional

Rhythm: samba
Tempo: medium (♩ = 108)
Synchro-start: on

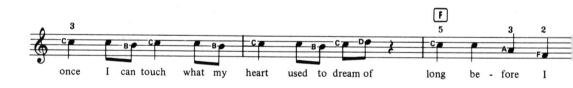

make my dream come true. For once in my life I won't

let sor - row hurt me —— not like it's hurt me be - fore. For

once I have some -thing I know won't de - sert me, and I'm not a - lone an - y -

more. For once I can say this is mine, you can take it, ——

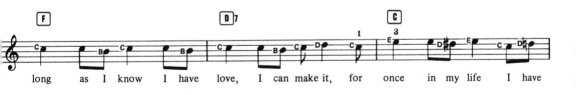

long as I know I have love, I can make it, for once in my life I have

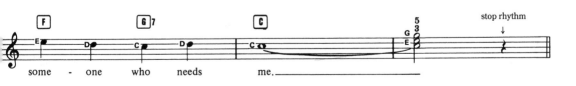

some - one who needs me. ——

ROCK AROUND THE CLOCK

Words & Music by Max C. Freedman & Jimmy de Knight

Suggested registration: trumpet, or saxophone
Rhythm: swing
Tempo: fairly fast (♩ = 160)

Press rhythm start button (ordinary, not synchro) with left hand, as right hand strikes first note. Play through Verse using melody and drums only. Start left hand chords at Chorus.

VERSE

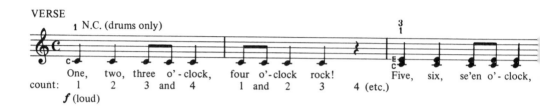

One, two, three o'-clock, four o'-clock rock! Five, six, se'en o'-clock,
count: 1 2 3 and 4 1 and 2 3 4 (etc.)
f (loud)

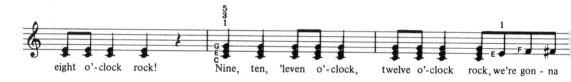

eight o'-clock rock! Nine, ten, 'leven o'-clock, twelve o'-clock rock, we're gon - na

CHORUS

rock a - round the clock to - night! Put your glad rags on,

join me hon, we'll have some fun when the clock strikes one, we're gon - na

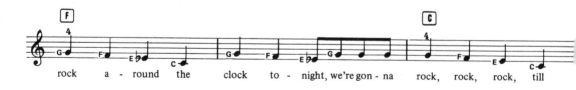

rock a - round the clock to - night, we're gon - na rock, rock, rock, till

broad day - light, we're gon - na rock, gon - na rock a - round the clock to -

add arpeggio (if available)

night._____ When the clock strikes two,

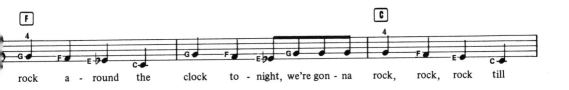

three and four, if the band slows down we'll yell for more, we're gon - na

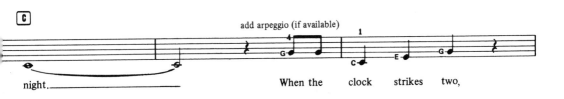

rock a - round the clock to - night, we're gon - na rock, rock, rock till

broad day - light, we're gon - na rock, gon - na rock a - round the clock to -

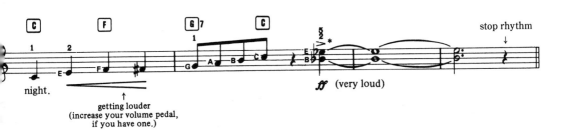

night.

getting louder
(increase your volume pedal,
if you have one.)

stop rhythm

ff (very loud)

* **ACCENT**

2 TWO NEW CHORDS: C7 AND A7

Using single-finger chord method:

Locate "C" and "A" in the accompaniment section of your keyboard. Convert these notes into C 7 and A 7 (see Part One , page 42ff., and your owner's manual).

Using fingered chord method:

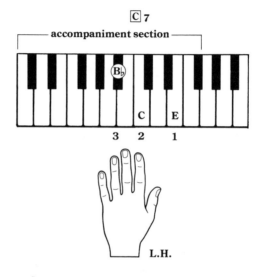

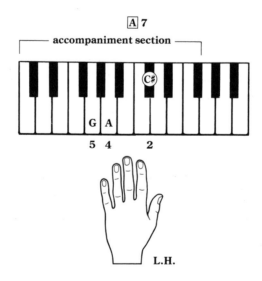

3 A NEW STAGE IN READING MUSIC

Up to now, in order to help you, letter names have appeared beside the written notes. These letters will now be discontinued.

Here's how you can learn the names of the notes:

The stave consists of five lines:-

remember this sentence:

Every **G**ood **B**oy **D**eserves **F**ruit

and four spaces:-

remember this word: **F A C E**

Learn the notes on the five lines, and the notes in the four spaces first. Then learn the "in-between" notes, like this:

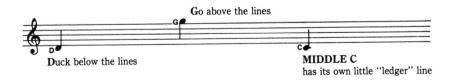

Go above the lines

Duck below the lines

MIDDLE C
has its own little "ledger" line

LOVE ME TENDER

Words & Music by Elvis Presley & Vera Matson

Suggested registration: string ensemble
Arpeggio optional

Rhythm: rhumba
Tempo: medium (♩ = 96)
Synchro-start: on

Love me ten - der, love me sweet, nev - er let me

p (soft)

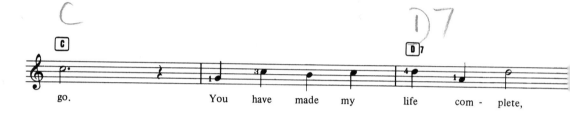

go. You have made my life com - plete,

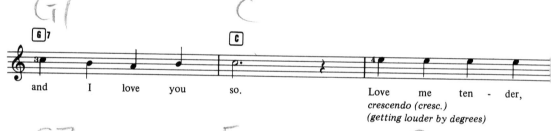

and I love you so. Love me ten - der,

crescendo (cresc.)
(getting louder by degrees)

love me true, all my dreams ful - fil.

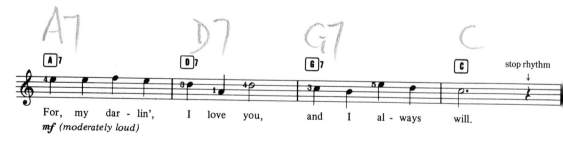

stop rhythm

For, my dar - lin', I love you, and I al - ways will.

mf (moderately loud)

TAKE THESE CHAINS FROM MY HEART

Words & Music by Fred Rose & Hy Heath

Suggested registration: guitar

Rhythm: 8 beat
Tempo: medium (♩ = 108)
Synchro-start: on

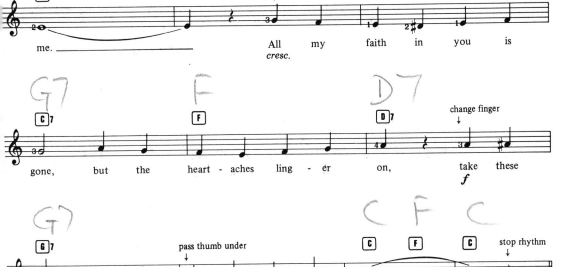

FORTUOSITY

Words & Music by Richard M. Sherman
& Robert B. Sherman

Suggested registration: trombone

Rhythm: swing
Tempo: fast (♩ = 200)
Synchro-start: on

For - tu - os - i - ty, that's me

by - word, for - tu - os - i - ty, the

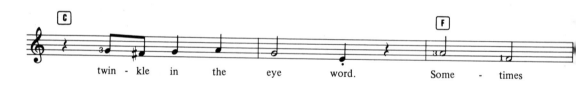

twin - kle in the eye word. Some - times

cas - tles fall to the ground, _____ but

that's where four - leaf clo - vers are found.

*TENUTO MARK. Hold the note for its full length.

For - tu - os - i - ty,

luck - y chan - ces, for - tu -

i - tious lit - tle hap - py hap - pen - stan - ces.

I don't wor - ry, 'cause ev - 'ry - where I

see that ev - 'ry bit of life is lit by

for - tu - os - i - ty!

*GRACE NOTES. Ornamental notes not included in the basic timing of the bar.
Play your grace notes as quickly as possible.

ARE YOU LONESOME TONIGHT

Words & Music by Roy Turk & Lou Handman

Suggested registration: flute + full sustain

Rhythm: waltz
Tempo: fairly slow (♩ = 92)
Synchro-start: on

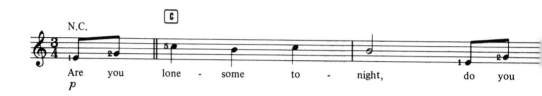

Are you lone - some to - night, do you

miss me to - night, are you sor - ry we

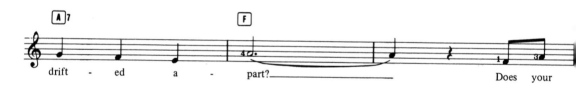

drift - ed a - part?_____ Does your

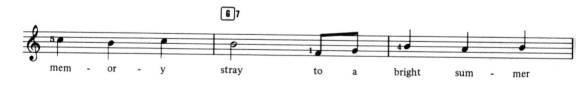

mem - or - y stray to a bright sum - mer

day, when I kissed you and called you "Sweet -

heart?" *mp cresc.* Do the chairs in your

during rest move 2nd finger up

par - lour seem emp - ty and bare, *mf* do you

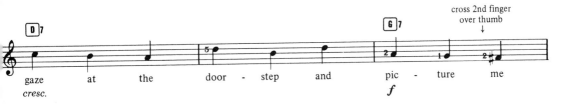

cross 2nd finger over thumb

cresc. gaze at the door - step and pic - ture me *f*

during rest, move hand up

there? *mp* Is your heart filled with pain? Shall I *cresc.*

tuck thumb under 2nd finger

come back a - gain? *f* Tell me dear, are you

stop rhythm

lone - some to - night?_____

4

STANDARD REPEATING DEVICES

FIRST AND SECOND TIME BARS:

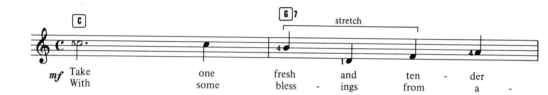

> 1.
> play these bars on the first time through only.

> 2.
> play this bar on the second
> time through, then carry on.

DA CAPO (D.C.)   from the beginning.

DA CAPO AL FINE (D.C. al Fine)   Go back to the beginning of the piece and
play through again until FINE (the end).

MEMORIES ARE MADE OF THIS

Words & Music by Terry Gilkyson, Richard Dehr & Frank Miller

Suggested registration: violin

Rhythm: swing
Tempo: fairly fast (♩ = 144)
Synchro-start: on

Take / With   one / some   fresh / bless - ings   and / ten - der / a -

kiss. / bove.   Add / Serve   one / it

sto - len / gen - 'rous - ly   night / of   of / with   bliss. / love.

One / One   girl, / man,   one / one   boy, / wife,

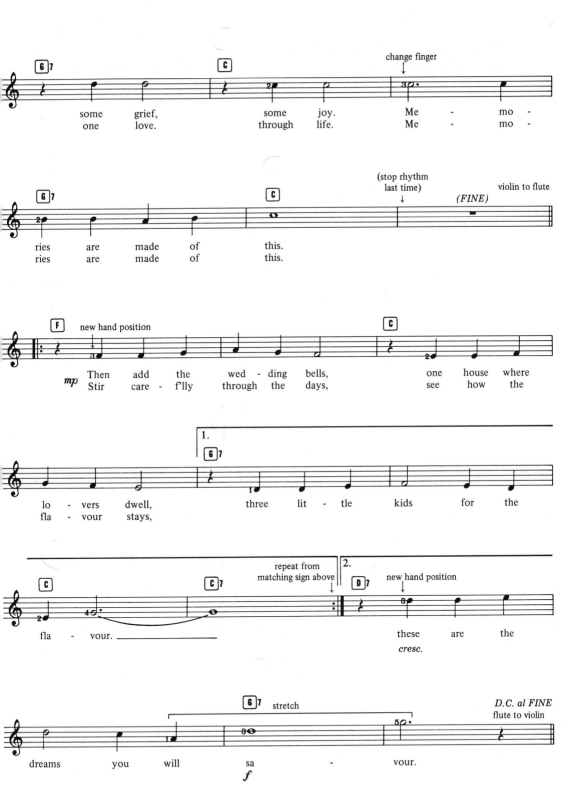

some grief,   some joy.   Me - mo -
one love.   through life.   Me - mo -

ries are made of this.
ries are made of this.

mp Then add the wed - ding bells,   one house where
Stir care - f'lly through the days,   see how the

lo - vers dwell,   three lit - tle kids for the
fla - vour stays,

fla - vour.   these are the
cresc.

dreams you will sa - vour.
f

5

THREE NEW NOTES FOR RIGHT HAND: LOW G, A, B

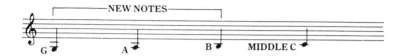

NEW NOTES

G   A   B   MIDDLE C

These three notes lie directly to the left of Middle C. The lowest of them, G, probably forms the left hand extremity of the "melody section" on your instrument.

I have placed letter names beside the new notes only in the next few songs.

GUANTANAMERA

Words by Jose Marti
Music adaptation by Hector Angulo & Peter Seeger

Suggested registration: pan flute

Rhythm: bossa nova
Tempo: medium (♩ = 112)
Synchro-start: on

cre - ce la pal - ma.___ Yo soy un hom - bre sin - ce - ro___

De don - de cre - ce la pal - ma___ Y an - tes de

mo - rir - me quie - ro, E - char mis ver - sos del al -

ma. Guan - ta - na - me - ra___ gua - ji - ra

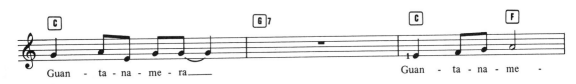

Guan - ta - na - me - ra___ Guan - ta - na - me -

ra, gua - ji - ra Guan - ta - na - me - ra!

CANDLE IN THE WIND

Words & Music by Elton John & Bernie Taupin

Suggested registration: clarinet

Rhythm: 8 beat
Tempo: medium (♩ = 120)
Synchro-start: on

VERSE

Good - bye Nor - ma Jean, ___ though I ne - ver knew you at all, ___
count: 1   2   3   4   and   1   2   3   and   4   and   1   2   3   4   and

— you had the grace to hold your - self, while those a - round you crawled..
1   2   3   and   4   and (etc.)

squeeze together

thumb under 2nd finger

They crawled out of the wood - work, ___

— and they whis - pered in - to your brain, they set you on a

tread - mill, and they made you change your name. ___

CHORUS
clarinet to trumpet

And it seems to me you lived your life like a

can - dle in the wind, _____ ne - ver know - ing who to

cling to when the rain set in. _____ And I

change finger

would have liked to have known you, but I was just a kid, your

can - dle had burned out long be - fore your le - gend e - ver did. _____
diminuendo (dim.)
(getting softer by degrees)

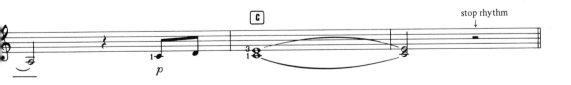

stop rhythm

WHEELS

Words by Norman Petty
Music by Jimmy Torres & Richard Stephens

Suggested registration: marimba (or xylophone)

Rhythm: cha-cha
Tempo: medium (♩ = 116)
Synchro-start: on

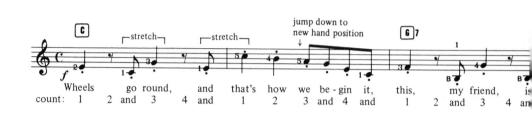

Wheels go round, and that's how we be-gin it, this, my friend, is
count: 1 2 and 3 4 and 1 2 3 and 4 and 1 2 and 3 4 an

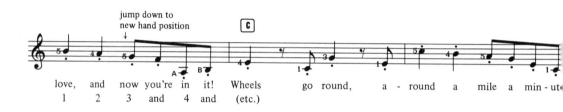

love, and now you're in it! Wheels go round, a - round a mile a min-ute
1 2 3 and 4 and (etc.)

fun - ny lit - tle wheels in - side your heart! Till it's done, there'l

be no way o' know - in' where you'll run, or why you're all a - glow - in'

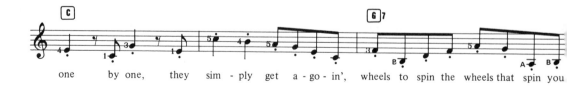

one by one, they sim - ply get a - go - in', wheels to spin the wheels that spin you

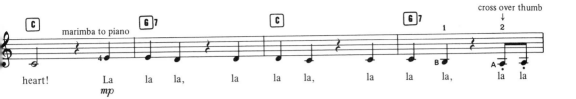

heart! La la la, la la la, la la la, la la

mp

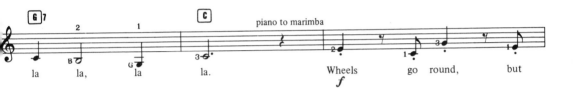

la la. La la la, la la la, la

la la, la la. Wheels go round, but

f

they don't cost a pen - ny, wheels go round, where once we had - n't a - ny.

Wheels that sound as though there's more than ma - ny, fun - ny lit - tle wheels in - side your

heart! Fun - ny lit - tle wheels in - side your heart!

ff

MINOR CHORDS

The MINOR CHORD is another important type of chord.

When using the single-finger chord function, there are various ways of forming minor chords. Your owner's manual will tell you how to form minor chords on your particular instrument. The first two diagrams below show two possibilities.

CHORD OF F MINOR Fm

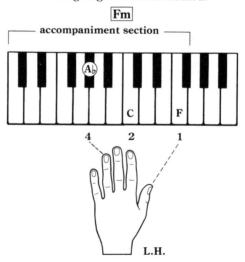

Using single-finger chord method:

Play F, together with any black note to its LEFT.

or:

Play F, together with any (one) note to its RIGHT.

Using fingered chord method:

7 DOTTED TIME NOTES

A dot after a note adds half as much time again to that note:-

		lasting
♩	half note (minim)	2 beats
♩.	dotted half note (dotted minim)	2 + 1 = 3 beats
♩	quarter note (crotchet)	1 beat
♩.	dotted quarter note (dotted crotchet)	1 + 1/2 = 1 1/2 beats

DOTTED QUARTER NOTE (DOTTED CROTCHET)

A Dotted Quarter Note, ♩. , worth 1 1/2 beats, usually combines with an Eighth Note (Quaver), ♪, worth 1/2 beat, to make two whole beats:-

or:

♩. ♪   1 1/2 + 1/2 = 2 beats

♪ ♩.   1/2 + 1 1/2 = 2 beats

The first of these two time note combinations: ♩. ♪ is the more common.

This is how you can count it:-

WHAT KIND OF FOOL AM I, page 76

| count: | (1) | What 2 | kind 3 | of 4 | fool 1 | am 2 and | I 3 | 4 |

Notice how the "dot" delays note D, so that the next note (E) falls on an "and" beat. The situation is always the same with this rhythm.

Look out for other examples of dotted quarter note/quaver combinations in the songs which follow.

WHAT KIND OF FOOL AM I

Words & Music by Leslie Bricusse & Anthony Newley

Suggested registration: piano & strings

Rhythm: rhumba
Tempo: medium (♩ = 108)
Synchro-start: on

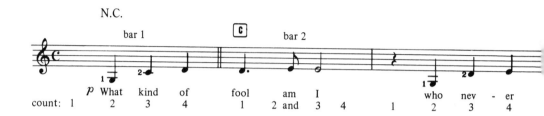

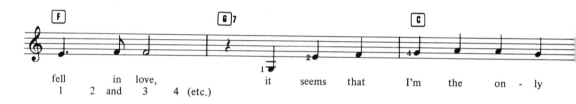

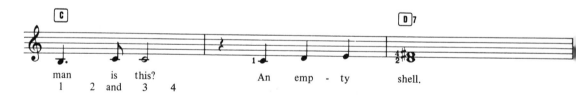

LAST OF THE SUMMER WINE

Composed by Ronnie Hazlehurst

Suggested registration: harmonica

Rhythm: waltz
Tempo: medium (♩ = 88)
Synchro-start: on

*HIGH A (see page 40).

STARDUST

Words by Mitchell Parish
Music by Hoagy Carmichael

Suggested registration: vibraphone, or celeste,
  + full sustain

Rhythm: swing
Tempo: fairly slow (♩ = 80)
Synchro-start: on

Some-times I won - der why I spend the lone - ly

count: 1 2 3 and 4 and 1 2 3 4 (etc.)

night dream-ing of a song, the mel - o - dy

haunts my re - ve - rie. And I am once a - gain with you. When our

love was new, and each kiss an in - spi - ra - tion

But that was long a - go, now my con - so - la - tion is

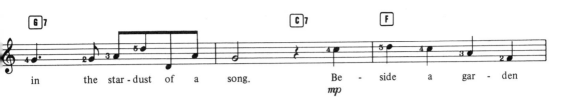

in the star-dust of a song. Be - side a gar - den

wall when stars are bright, you are in my arms. The

night - in - gale tells his fai - ry tale of par - a -dise where ro -ses

tuck 5th finger
around 4th
↓

grew. Tho' I dream in vain, in my

cresc.

tuck thumb
under 2nd finger
↓

stretch

heart it will re - main. My star-dust mel - o - dy,

ƒ

stop rhythm
↓

the mem - o - ry of love's re - frain.

8 CHORD OF D MINOR [Dm], AND CHORD OF A MINOR [Am]

Using single-finger chord method:

Locate D (the higher one), and A, in the accompaniment section of your keyboard. Convert these notes into [Dm] and [Am] respectively (see page 76 and your owner's manual).

Using fingered chord method:

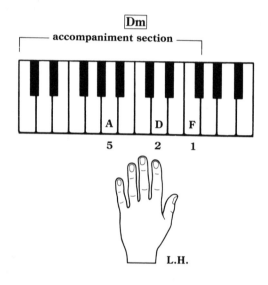

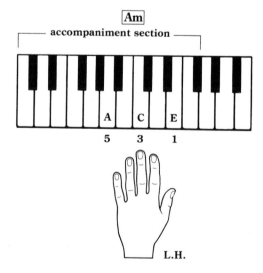

SCARBOROUGH FAIR

Traditional

Suggested registration: harpsichord

Rhythm: waltz
Tempo: slow ($\quad$ = 88)
Synchro-start: on

Are you go - ing to Scar - bor - ough

p

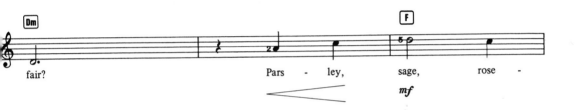

fair? Pars - ley, sage, rose -

mf

ma - ry and thyme Re -

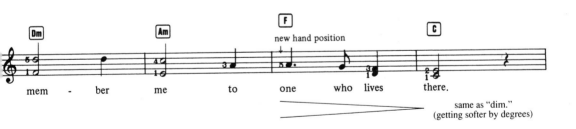

new hand position

mem - ber me to one who lives there.

same as "dim."
(getting softer by degrees)

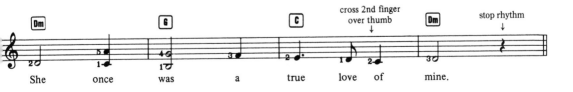

cross 2nd finger
over thumb

stop rhythm

She once was a true love of mine.

TAKE ME HOME, COUNTRY ROADS

Words & Music by Bill Danoff, Taffy Nivert & John Denver

Suggested registration: electric piano

Rhythm: swing
Tempo: quite fast (♩ = 192)
Synchro-start: on

Almost heaven, West Virginia,

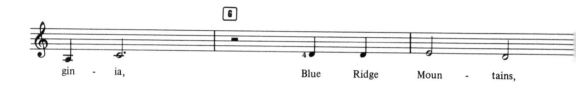

ginia, Blue Ridge Mountains,

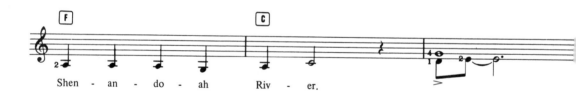

Shenandoah River.

Life is old there, older than the

trees, younger than the mountains

THREE NEW NOTES FOR RIGHT HAND: HIGH A, B, C

If you have a 44, or a 49 note keyboard, these will be your top three notes.

I have placed letter names beside the new notes in the next few songs.

SAILING

Words & Music by Gavin Sutherland

Suggested registration: jazz organ + sustain
Rhythm: disco
Tempo: slow (♩ = 69); but run at double speed (♩ = 138)

I am sail - ing, I am sail - ing, home a -

gain _____ 'cross the sea. I am sail - ing storm-y

wa - ters to be near _____ you, to be free. I am

*Pause on each note, for dramatic effect.

SPANISH EYES

Words by Charles Singleton & Eddie Snyder
Music by Bert Kaempfert

Suggested registration: steel drums

Rhythm: beguine
Tempo: medium (♩ = 108)
Synchro-start: on

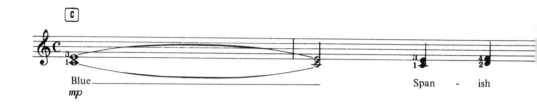

Blue _____ Span - ish

mp

eyes, _____ tear - drops are fall - ing

cresc.

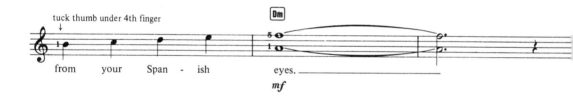

tuck thumb under 4th finger

from your Span - ish eyes. _____

mf

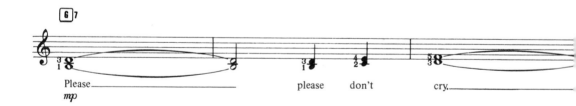

Please _____ please don't cry. _____

mp

_____ This is just a - dios and not good

cresc.

88

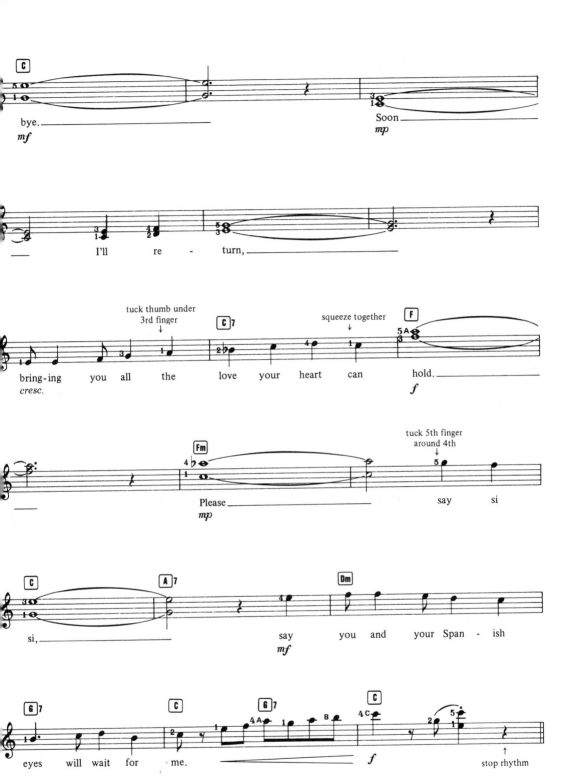

bye._____ Soon____

mf *mp*

____ I'll re - turn,_____

tuck thumb under
3rd finger

squeeze together

bring-ing you all the love your heart can hold.____

cresc. *f*

tuck 5th finger
around 4th

____ Please _____ say si

mp

si,_____ say you and your Span - ish

mf

eyes will wait for me._____ *f* stop rhythm

HOW DEEP IS YOUR LOVE

Words & Music by Barry Gibb, Robin Gibb,
& Maurice Gibb

Suggested registration: flute

Rhythm: rock
Tempo: medium (♩ = 108)
Synchro-start: on

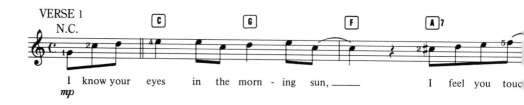

I know your eyes in the morn - ing sun, _____ I feel you touc

_ me in the pour - ing rain. _____ And the mo - ment that you wan - der

far from me, _____ I wan - na feel you in my arms a - gain. _____ And you

come to me _ on a sum-mer breeze,_keep me warm in your love, _ then you

soft - ly leave, and it's me you need to show. _____ How

deep is your love?_ How deep is your love? I real-ly mean_ to

new hand position

new hand position

learn, _ 'cause we're liv-ing in a world of fools, _ break-ing us

down, when they all should let us be. We be -

cut piano

mp

long to you and me, I be-lieve in you, _ you know the door_

_ to my ve - ry soul. _ You're the light _ in my deep - est

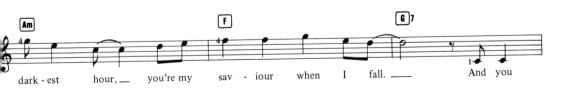

dark-est hour, _ you're my sav - iour when I fall. _ And you

may not think ___ I care for you, ___ when you know down in - side ___ that I

real - ly do. And it's me you need to show. ___ How

f

deep is your love? ___ How deep is your love? I real - ly mean ___ to

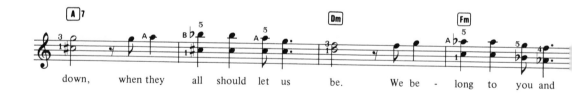

learn, ___ 'cause we're liv - ing in a world of fools, ___ break - ing us

down, when they all should let us be. We be - long to you and

play 3 times

me.

HELLO GOODBYE

Words & Music by John Lennon & Paul McCartney

Suggested registration: synth brass

Rhythm: rock
Tempo: medium (♩ = 112)
Synchro-start: on

You say yes___ I say no___ you say stop___ and
mp

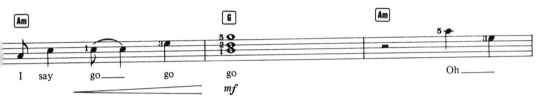

I say go___ go go Oh___

no. You say good - bye, and I say hel -
mp

lo, Hel - lo, hel - lo. I don't know why you say good-bye, I say hel -
cresc.

lo, Hel - lo, hel - lo. I don't know why you say good-bye, I say hel - lo.
mf *f* rit

LAST WORD

Congratulations on reaching the end of Part Two of 'The Complete Keyboard Player'.

In Part Three you will:

- improve your note reading
- learn new chords
- play in new keys, including "minor" keys
- develop further your sense of rhythm
- add those important professional touches to your playing.

CHORD CHART (Showing all "fingered chords" used in the course so far)

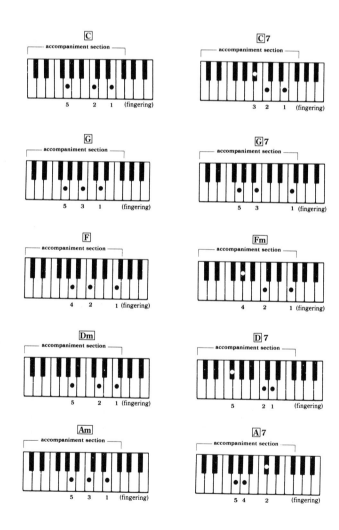

The Complete Keyboard Player

by **Kenneth Baker**

In Part Three of The Complete Keyboard Player you learn about scales and keys.
When you play in different keys you make basic changes of sound, and so add a
new dimension to your playing. Minor keys, especially, can change the whole flavour of
your music. In Part Three you play in five new keys, including two minor keys.

In Part Three you continue your left hand studies, with the emphasis as usual on
'fingered' chords. Nine new chords are introduced, in easy stages, and all the chords used
in the series appear in the Chord Chart at the back of the book.

There is plenty for your right hand in Part Three. There are double notes, chords,
fill-ins and counter-melodies.

As usual, throughout the book you will get tips on how to use the facilities of the
keyboard - the sounds, the rhythms, and so on-more effectively.

Although Part Three continues in the 'teach yourself' tradition of the earlier books,
all teachers of the instrument will want to make it one of their standard text books.

The optional matching CD or cassette, on which you can hear the author playing all
the songs from the book, will help you to learn even faster!

CHORD OF E7

Using single-finger chord method:

Locate "E" (the higher one of two) in the accompaniment section of your keyboard. Convert this note into E 7 (see Part One , page 42ff., and your owner's manual).

Using fingered chord method:

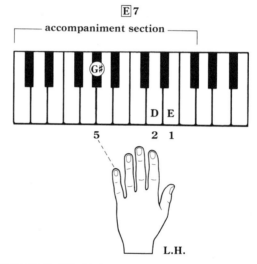

THE WINNER TAKES IT ALL

Words & Music by Benny Andersson & Bjorn Ulvaeus

Suggested registration: piano

Rhythm: rock
Tempo: medium (♩ = 112)
Synchro-start: on

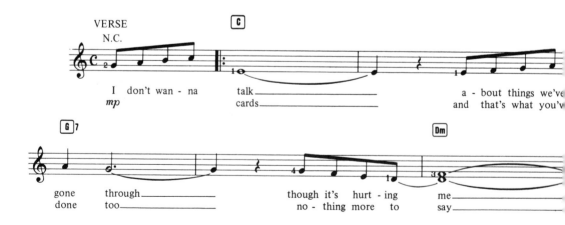

VERSE
N.C.

I don't wan - na talk_____ a - bout things we've
cards_____ and that's what you'v

mp

gone through_____ though it's hurt - ing me_____
done too_____ no - thing more to say_____

now it's his - to - ry. I've played all my
no more ace to play.

CHORUS

2. change piano to brass ensemble
The win - ner takes it all, the lo - ser stand - ing

small be - side the vic - to - ry,

that's her des - ti - ny. The game is on a -

gain, a lov - er or a friend,

a big thing or a small the win - ner takes it

all.

I LEFT MY HEART IN SAN FRANCISCO

Words by Douglas Cross
Music by George Cory

Suggested registration: string ensemble

Rhythm: swing
Tempo: fairly slow (♩ = 96)
Synchro-start: on

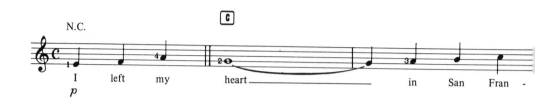

I left my heart _____ in San Fran -

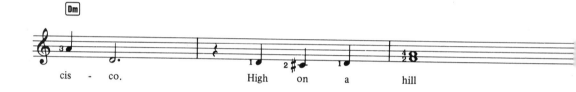

cis - co. High on a hill

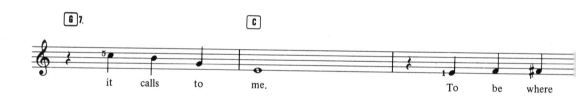

it calls to me. To be where

lit - tle ca - ble cars _____ climb half - way to the stars.

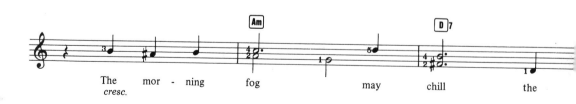

The mor - ning fog may chill the

air,   I   don't   care!   My   love   waits   there___

mf   *p*

___   in   San   Fran - cis - co.   A -   bove   the

blue   and   wind - y   sea.

cresc.   *f*

When   I   come   home   to   you,   San   Fran -

cis - co.   Your   gold - en   sun   will

stop rhythm

shine   for   me.   *ff*

2 CHORD OF E MINOR Em

Using single-finger chord method:

Locate "E" (the higher one of two) in the accompaniment section of your keyboard. Convert this note into Em (see Part Two, page 76, and your owner's manual).

Using fingered chord method:

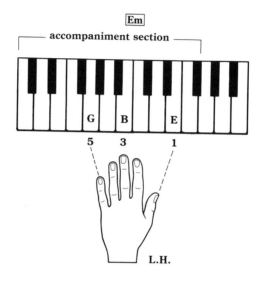

BRIGHT EYES

Words & Music by Mike Batt

Suggested registration: electric guitar + arpeggio
Rhythm: rock
Tempo: medium ($\quarternote$ = 96)
Synchro-start: on

VERSE C F C

Is it a kind of a dream._____
fog a-long the ho - ri - zon.

Am F C

Float - ing out on the tide._____
Cold sound in the air._____

Fol - low-ing the riv - er of death down - stream.
No - bo - dy ev - er knows when you go,

Oh is it a
and where do you

1.
(when there is no matching repeat sign, repeat from the beginning of the piece) 2.

dream?

There's a start, Oh, oh,

CHORUS

is it a dream?

Bright ___
f

eyes, burn - ing like ___ fire ___

___ Bright ___ eyes how can you close ___ and

fail.

How can the light ___ that burned so bright - ly

stop rhythm

sud - den - ly burn ___ so pale? Bright ___ eyes. ___

THE SONG FROM "MOULIN ROUGE"

(WHERE IS YOUR HEART?)

Words by William Engvick
Music by Georges Auric

Suggested registration: hawaiian guitar

Rhythm: waltz
Tempo: slow (♩ = 88)
Synchro-start: on

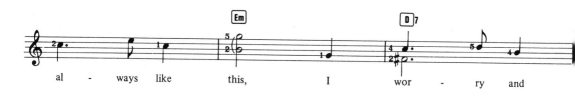

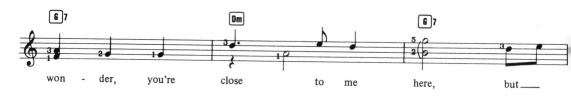

*Split these two notes (playing lower note first).

where is your heart? It's a sad thing to re - al -

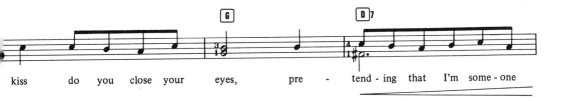

ise that you've a heart that nev - er melts. _____ When we

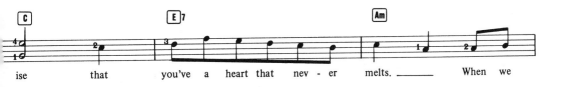

kiss do you close your eyes, pre - tend - ing that I'm some - one

else? You must break the spell, this

mf   *mp*

cloud that I'm un - der, so please won't you

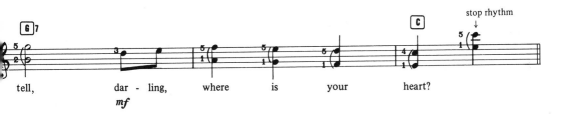

tell, dar - ling, where is your heart?

mf

SCALE OF C; KEY OF C

A scale is a succession of adjoining notes:

Scale of C (major)

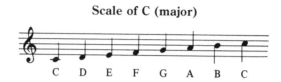

As you see, there are no black notes in the scale of C.

When a piece is built on this scale it is said to be in the "key of C". Almost all the pieces you have played so far have been in the key of C. The occasional black notes you encountered in those pieces were of a temporary nature only, and did not affect the overall key.

From now on you are going to play in a number of different keys for the sake of contrast.

SCALE OF F; KEY OF F

Scale of F (major)

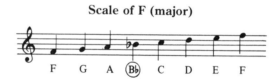

As you see, a B Flat is required to form the scale of F. When you are playing in this key, therefore, you must remember to play all your B's, wherever they might fall on the keyboard, as B Flats.

To remind you, a B Flat is inserted at the beginning of every line:-

key signature

To help you further, I have arrowed the first few B Flats in the following songs.

CHORD OF B♭ ; CHORD OF F 7

You need these two chords in order to play in the Key of F.

Using single-finger chord method:

Locate "B♭" in the accompaniment section of your keyboard. Play this note on its own and you will have a chord of B♭ (major).

Locate "F" (the lower one of two) in the accompaniment section of your keyboard. Convert this into F 7 (see Part One , page 42ff., and your owner's manual).

Using fingered chord method:

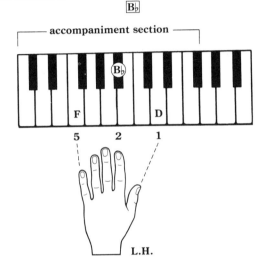

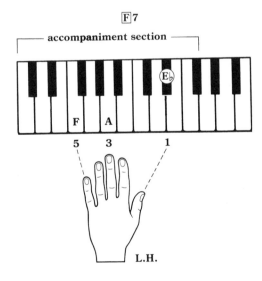

OB-LA-DI, OB-LA-DA

Words & Music by John Lennon & Paul McCartney

Suggested registration: funny

Rhythm: swing
Tempo: fast (♩ = 112)
Synchro-start: on

Des - mond has a bar - row in the

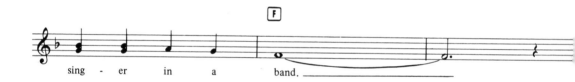

mar - ket place____ Mol - ly is the

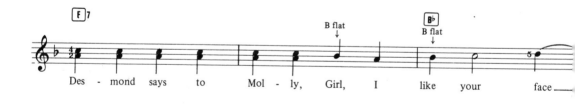

sing - er in a band. ____

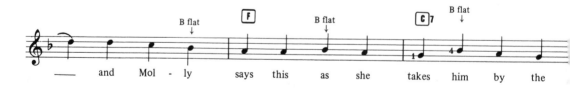

Des - mond says to Mol - ly, Girl, I like your face____

____ and Mol - ly says this as she takes him by the

*Cut Common Time. A feeling of two in a bar (²⁄₂) rather than four (⁴⁄₄).
Notice the metronome marking: ♩ = 112.

106

CHORUS

hand _____ Ob la di, ob la

ff

da, life goes on, bra,

la la how the life goes on. _____

_____ Ob la di, ob la da, life goes

on, bra, la la how the

life goes on. stop rhythm

FALLING

Words & Music by Angelo Badalamenti & David Lynch

Suggested registration: guitar

Rhythm: rock
Tempo: slow (♩ = 100)
Synchro-start: on

INTRO.

add string ensemble
VERSE 1

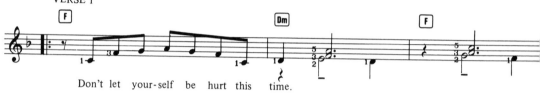

Don't let your-self be hurt this time.

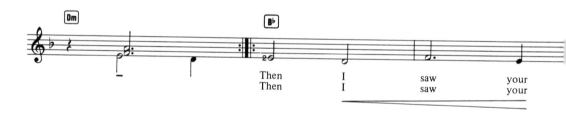

Then   I   saw   your
Then   I   saw   your

face.
smile

VERSE 2

The   sky   is   still   blue,   the

clouds come ____ and go, but some - thing ____ is

diff - 'rent, ____ are we fall - ing in

p cresc.

love?

mf

CHORUS

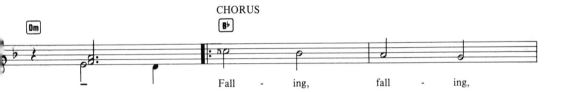

Fall - ing, fall - ing,

fall - ing, fall - ing in love.

(Repeat and Fade)

TULIPS FROM AMSTERDAM

English Words by Gene Martyn
Original Words by Neumann and Bader
Music by Ralf Arnie

Suggested registration: accordion

Rhythm: waltz
Tempo: fast (♩ = 184)
Synchro-start: on

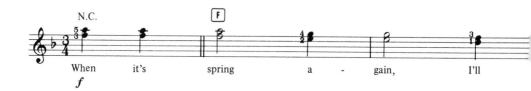

When it's spring a - gain, I'll

bring a - gain Tu - lips from

Am - ster - dam. With a

heart that's true I'll give to you

Tu - lips from Am - ster - dam. I can't

wait   un - til   the   day   you   fill

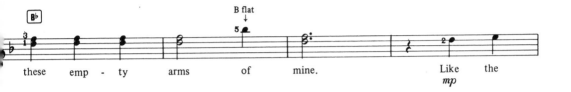

these   emp - ty   arms   of   mine.   Like   the

mp

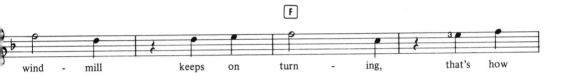

wind - mill   keeps   on   turn - ing,   that's   how

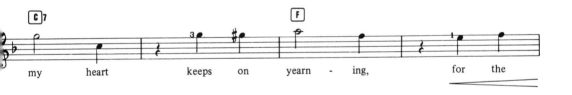

my   heart   keeps   on   yearn - ing,   for   the

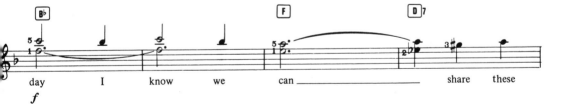

day   I   know   we   can ——————————   share   these

f

Tu - lips   from   Am - ster - dam.

ff

4 TRIPLETS

A triplet is a group of 3 notes played in the time of 2:-

Eighth Note (Quaver) Triplets must be played slightly FASTER than normal eighth notes, in order to fit them to the beat. Compare the following two examples:-

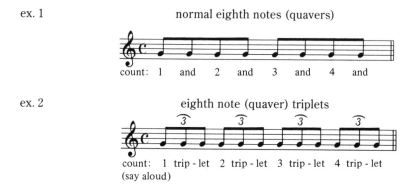

ex. 1   normal eighth notes (quavers)

count: 1   and   2   and   3   and   4   and

ex. 2   eighth note (quaver) triplets

count: 1 trip - let   2 trip - let   3 trip - let   4 trip - let
(say aloud)

If you incorporate the word "triplet" into your counting like this, you will get the feeling of the triplets.

SIXTEENTH NOTES (SEMIQUAVERS), AND DOTTED RHYTHMS

An eighth note (quaver) can be subdivided into two sixteenth notes (semiquavers):-

eighth note   sixteenth notes

"dotted" eighth note is equal to half as much again (see "dotted time notes", book Two, page 29), that is, three sixteenth notes:-

dotted eighth note   sixteenth notes

practice, a dotted eighth note usually pairs up with a sixteenth note:-

dotted eighth note sixteenth note

together these two time notes are equivalent to 4 sixteenth notes, or quarter note (crotchet):-

3 sixteenth notes + 1 sixteenth note = quarter note

he general effect of a passage like:-

of eighth notes (quavers) with a "lilt". The phrase "humpty dumpty" can be used s a guide to this rhythm:-

say: hump - ty dump - ty hump - ty dump - ty

stress

hese uneven types of rhythms are often called "Dotted Rhythms". Look out for otted rhythms in the next four pieces.

In *Close To You*, watch out for "normal" eighth notes, eighth note triplets, and dotted rhythms.

(THEY LONG TO BE) CLOSE TO YOU

Words by Hal David. Music by Burt Bacharach

Suggested registration: piano

Rhythm: swing
Tempo: medium (♩ = 96)
Synchro-start: on

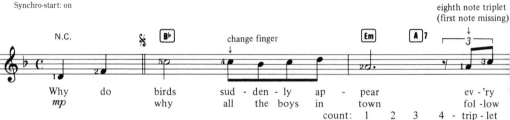

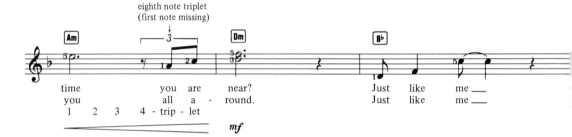

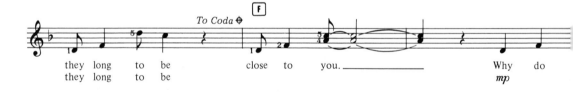

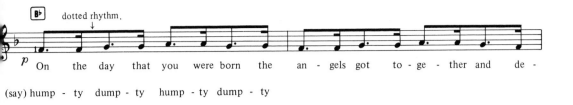

p On the day that you were born the an - gels got to - ge - ther and de -

(say) hump - ty dump - ty hump - ty dump - ty

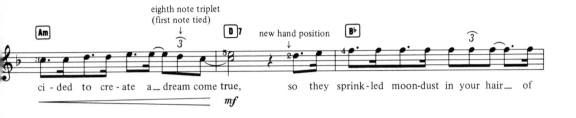

ci - ded to cre - ate a— dream come true, so they sprink-led moon-dust in your hair— of

mf

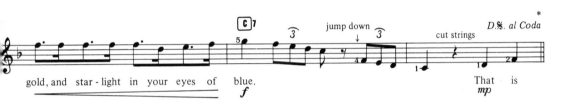

gold, and star - light in your eyes of blue. That is

f *mp*

▸ *CODA*

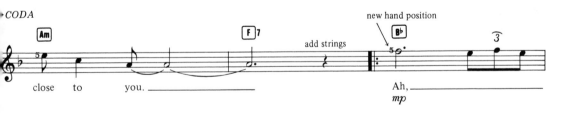

close to you. _____ Ah, _____

mp

_____ close to you. _____

*A **CODA** is a section, usually quite short, added to a piece of music to make an ending.
DAL SEGNO AL CODA (*D.S. al CODA*) means go back to the sign: 𝄋 and play through the same music again, until: "*to CODA* ⊕". From here jump to *CODA* and play through to the end.

5 SCALE OF G; KEY OF G

Scale of G (major)

An F Sharp is required to form the scale of G. When a piece is built on this scale it is said to be in the "key of G". When you are playing in this key you must remember to play all Fs, wherever they might fall on the keyboard, as F Sharps. The key signature, which appears at the beginning of every line, will remind you:-

key signature   Key of G

CHORD OF B7

Using single-finger chord method:

Locate "B" in the accompaniment section of your keyboard. Convert this into B7 (see Part One, page 42ff., and your owner's manual).

Using fingered chord method:

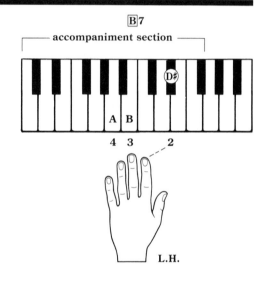

CHANSON D'AMOUR
Words & Music by Wayne Shanklin

Suggested registration: choir

Rhythm: swing
Tempo: medium (♩ = 100)
Synchro-start: on

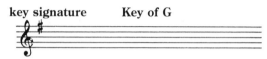

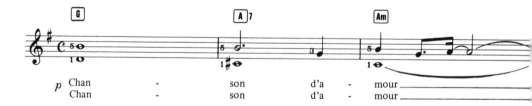

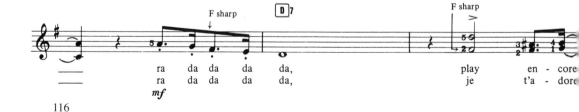

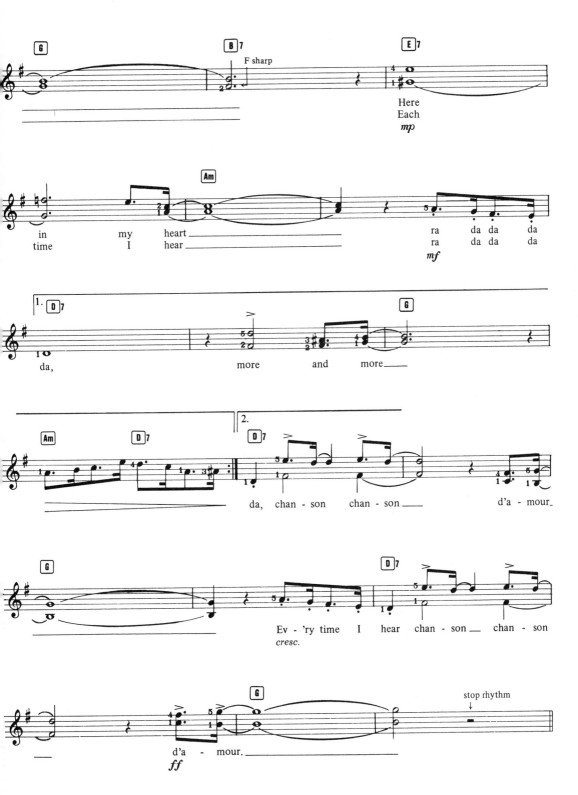

117

WHEN I'M SIXTY-FOUR

Words & Music by John Lennon & Paul McCartney

Suggested registration: clarinet

Rhythm: swing
Tempo: medium (♩ = 112)
Synchro-start: on

When I get old - er, los - ing my hair __ ma - ny __ years from

now, will you still be send - ing me a Val - en - tine __

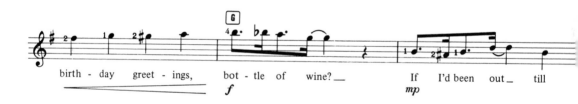

birth - day greet - ings, bot - tle of wine? __ If I'd been out __ till

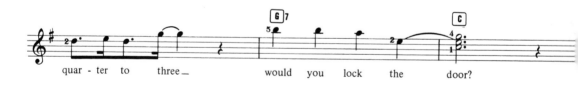

quar - ter to three __ would you lock the door?

Will you still need __ me, will you still feed __ me, when I'm six - ty __

118

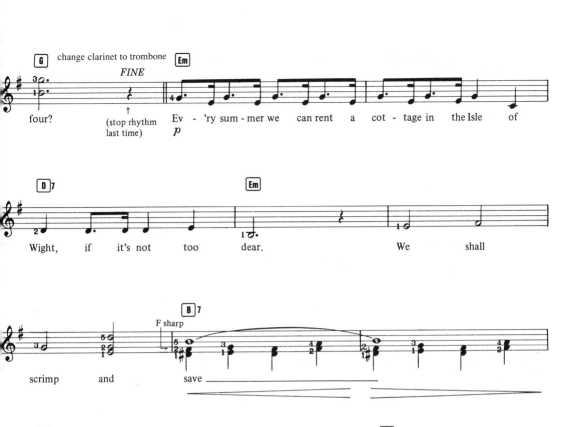

four? (stop rhythm last time) *p* Ev - 'ry sum - mer we can rent a cot - tage in the Isle of

Wight, if it's not too dear. We shall

scrimp and save _____

Ah _____ grand - child - ren on your knee_____

_____ Ve - ra, Chuck, and

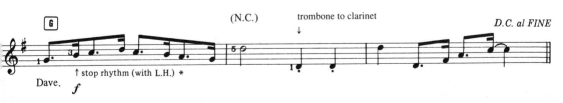

Dave. *f* ↑ stop rhythm (with L.H.) *

*Leave synchro button on, and rhythm will start again automatically when you strike the next chord ("G", at the beginning of the piece).

CHORDS OF G MINOR Gm , AND B♭ MINOR B♭m

Using single-finger chord method:

Locate "G" and "B♭" in the accompaniment section of your keyboard. Convert these notes into Gm and B♭m respectively (see Part Two , page 74, and your owner's manual).

Using fingered chord method:

Gm

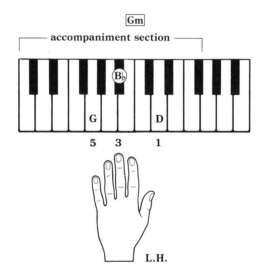

Compare this chord with G (major), a chord you already know.

B♭m

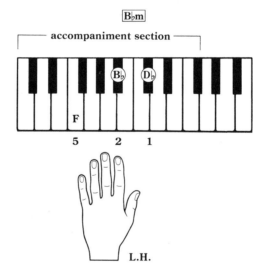

Compare this chord with B♭ (major), a chord you already know.

ISN'T SHE LOVELY

Words & Music by Stevie Wonder

Suggested registration: piano + sustain

Rhythm: swing
Tempo: medium (♩ = 112)
Synchro-start: on

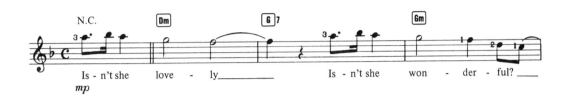

Is - n't she love - ly_____ Is - n't she won - der - ful? ____

mp

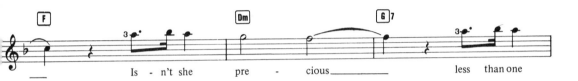

___ Is - n't she pre - cious_____ less than one

min - ute old?_____ I nev - er thought ___ through love we'd

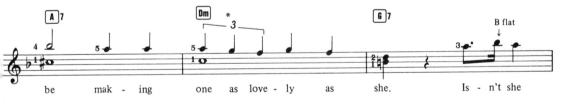

be mak - ing one as love - ly as she. Is - n't she

D.C. (Repeat and Fade)

love - ly, made from love. ___ Stop rhythm (with L.H.)

*QUARTER NOTE (CROTCHET) TRIPLET. 3 quarter notes played in the time of 2. Play these quarter notes slightly faster than usual, in order to fit them into the bar, but keep them even, and equal to each other.

(EVERYTHING I DO) I DO IT FOR YOU

Words & Music by Bryan Adams, R.J. Lange and M. Kamen

Suggested registration: flute

Rhythm: 8 beat
Tempo: slow (♩ = 80)
Synchro-start: on

Look in- to my eyes,   you will see _____   what you mean to

mp

me.   Search your heart, _____   search your soul, _____   and when you

flute to synth.

find me there you'll search no more. Don't tell me it's not worth try - in'

mf

for.   You can't tell me it's not worth dy - in' for.   You know it's

true, _____ ev- 'ry - thing I do, I do it for _____ you

p

synth. to flute

Look in - to your heart, you will find ___ no - thin' there to hide. Take me
mp

flute to synth.

as I am, take my life, ___ I would give it all I would sac - ri - fice. You can't

tell me it's not worth try - in' for. I can't help ___ it there's no - thin' I want
mf

more. Yeah, I would fight for you, I'd lie for you. Walk the

stop rhythm (then synchro-start on)
synth. to flute

(rhythm starts)

wire for you, ___ yeah, I'd die for you, you know it's true, ev - 'ry - thing I
f *mp*

stop rhythm

do, oh, ___ I do it for ___ you. ___
mf

7 MINOR KEYS

So far almost all your playing has been in major keys: C, F, and G. Songs written in minor keys, with their preponderance of minor chords, often have a sad, nostalgic quality, which makes an excellent contrast.

KEY OF D MINOR

The key of D Minor is related to the key of F Major. The scales on which these keys are built use the same notes:

Scale of D Minor ('natural')

D E F G A (B♭) C D

Scale of F

F G A (B♭) C D E F

All the notes are white except one: B Flat. As you would expect, both keys have the same key signature:

Key of D Minor

Key of F

When playing in the key of D Minor (as in the key of F), you must remember to play all B's, wherever they might fall on the keyboard, as B Flats.

SUNNY

Words & Music by Bobby Hebb

Suggested registration: *jazz organ, with stereo chorus.*

Rhythm: rock
Tempo: medium (♩ = 96)
Synchro-start: on

Sun - ny
mp

yes - ter - day my life was filled with

rain. Sun - ny

you smiled at me and

real - ly eased the pain, oh the dark days are done and the
cresc.

bright days are here, my Sun - ny one shines so sin - cere, oh, Sun - ny one so
mf

true, I love you.
1. *f*
2. *f*

HAVA NAGILA

Traditional

Suggested registration: bass clarinet
Rhythm: march $\frac{2}{4}$ (or swing)
Tempo: medium ($\quarternote$ = 112)

(Speed up tempo control, bit by bit, with left hand)

Change bass clarinet to
harpsichord 2nd time

(leave tempo control now)

Stop rhythm

KEY OF E MINOR

The key of E Minor is related to the key of G Major. Both keys use the same scale notes:

Scale of E Minor ('natural')

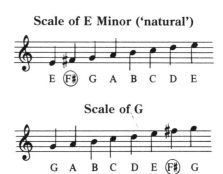

E (F♯) G A B C D E

Scale of G

G A B C D E (F♯) G

All the notes are white except one: F Sharp.

The key signature is the same for both keys:

Key of E Minor

Key of G

When playing in the key of E Minor (as in the key of G), you must remember to play all F's, wherever they might fall on the keyboard, as F Sharps.

CALLAN (SOGNO NOSTALGICO)

By Armando Sciascia

Suggested registration: guitar

Rhythm: waltz
Tempo: slow (♩ = 88)
Synchro-start: on

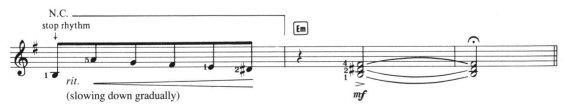

A WOMAN IN LOVE

Words & Music by Barry Gibb & Robin Gibb

Suggested registration: flute

Rhythm: 8 beat
Tempo: medium (♩ = 96)
Synchro-start: on

VERSES

1. Life is a mo-ment in space,__ when the dream is gone,__ it's a lone-li-er place.__
2. With you e-ter-nal-ly mine,__ in love there is__ no__ mea-sure of time.__

mp

__ I kiss the morn-ing good-bye,__ but down in - side__
__ We planned it all at the start,__ that you and I__

cresc.

__ you know we ne-ver know why.__ The road is nar-row and long,__
__ live in each oth-er's heart. *mf* We may be o-ceans a-way,__

mp

__ when eyes meet eyes,__ and the feel-ing is strong.__
__ you feel my love,__ I hear what you say.__

I turn a-way from the wall,__ I stum-ble and fall,__ but I give you it all.__
The truth is ev-er a lie,__ I stum-ble and fall,__ but I give you it all.__

cresc.

CHORUS

KEY OF B FLAT

The scale of B Flat, and therefore the key of B Flat, requires two flats: B Flat, and E Flat:-

Scale / Key of B Flat (major)

key signature

When you are playing in this key you must remember to play all B's and E's, wherever they might fall on the keyboard, as B Flats and E Flats, respectively.

CHORD OF E♭ (MAJOR)

Using single-finger chord method:

Play the note "E♭" (the higher one of two) in the accompaniment section of your keyboard.

Using fingered chord method:

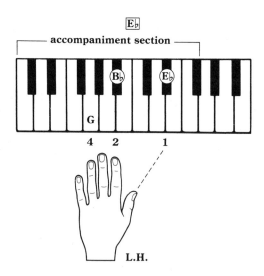

DON'T CRY FOR ME ARGENTINA

Music by Andrew Lloyd Webber
Lyrics by Tim Rice

Suggested registration: trumpet

Rhythm: tango
Tempo: medium (♩ = 112)
Synchro-start: on

Don't cry for me Ar - gen - ti - na, the truth is I nev - er

mp

left you. All through my wild days, my mad ex - ist - ence, I kept my

change trumpet
to clarinet

pro - mise, don't keep your dis - tance. ___ Don't cry for me Ar - gen -

ti - na, the truth is I nev - er left you. All through my

wild days, my mad ex - ist - ence, I kept my pro - mise, don't keep your

dis - tance. ___ *mf*

MAMMA MIA

Words & Music by Benny Andersson, Stig Anderson
& Bjorn Alvaeus

Suggested registration: oboe

Rhythm: rock
Tempo: medium (♩ = 126)
Synchro-start: on

I've been cheat-ed by you___ since I don't know when.
So I made up my mind___ it must come to an end.

Look at me now___ will I ev - er learn?

I don't know how___ but I sud - den - ly lose___ con - trol

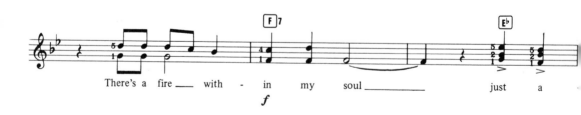

There's a fire ___ with - in my soul ___ just a

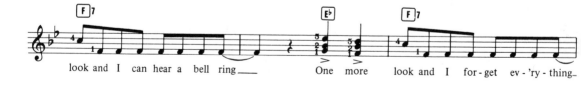

look and I can hear a bell ring ___ One more look and I for - get ev -'ry - thing___

CHORUS

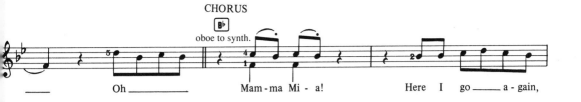

Oh _____ Mam-ma Mi - a! Here I go _____ a - gain,

my, my! How can I re - sist you? Mam-ma Mi - a!

Does it show _____ a - gain, my, my! Just how much I've missed you.

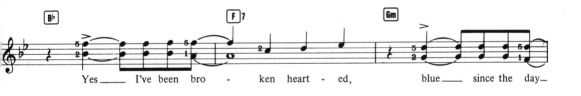

Yes _____ I've been bro - ken heart - ed, blue _____ since the day _____

_____ we part - ed, why, why, did I ev - er let _____ you

go?

ff

135

CHORD OF C MINOR [Cm]

Using single-finger chord method:

Locate "C" (the higher one of two) in the accompaniment section of your keyboard. Convert this note into [Cm] (see Part Two , page 76, and your owner's manual).

Using fingered chord method:

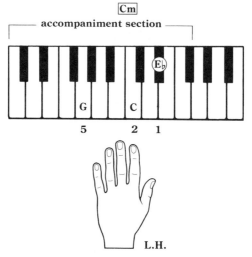

Compare this chord with [C] (major), a chord you already know.

RAINDROPS KEEP FALLING ON MY HEAD

Words by Hal David
Music by Burt Bacharach

Suggested registration: whistle

Rhythm: swing
Tempo: medium (♩ = 104)
Synchro-start: on

Rain - drops   keep fall - in' on   my   head,
did   me   some talk - in' to   the   sun.
mp

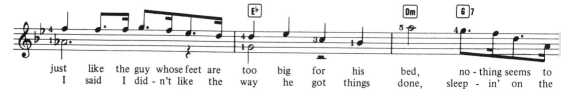

just   like   the guy whose feet are   too   big   for   his   bed,   no - thing seems to
I   said   I did - n't like the   way   he   got   things   done,   sleep - in' on the

To Coda ⊕

fit, those rain-drops are fall - in' on my head, they keep fall - in', __
job, those rain-drops are fall - in' on my head, they keep fall - in', __

whistle to vibes 2nd time

So I just
But there's one thing I know, the

blues they send to meet me won't de - feat me, it
cresc.

won't be long __ till hap - pi - ness steps up to greet __ me.

D.C. al Coda*

⊕ CODA

Be - cause I'm

stop rhythm

free _____ no-thin's wor-ry - ing me. __

*DA CAPO AL CODA (*D.C. al Coda*) means go back to the beginning of the piece and play through the same music again, until: "*to CODA* ⊕". From here jump to *CODA* and play through to the end.

STAR WARS (THEME)

By John Williams

Suggested registration: brass ensemble

Rhythm: disco
Tempo: medium (♩ = 112)
Synchro-start: on

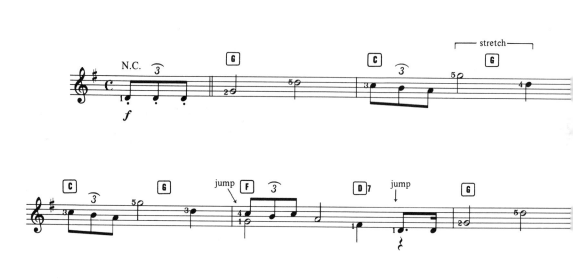

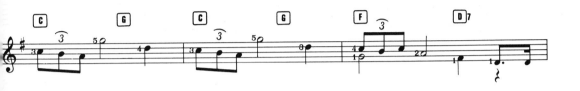

hold top note through this bar

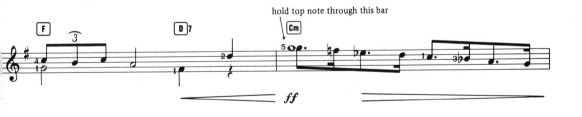

stop rhythm

CHORD CHART (Showing all "fingered chorus" used in the course so far)

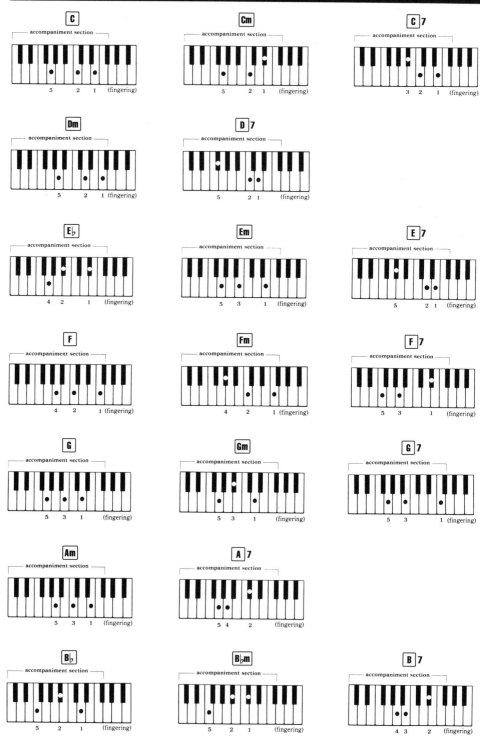

2/00(36644)